CULTIVATE THE MORNING CALM

Following Nature's Way to a Peaceful Life

Mary Mac

This book is for all Human Genius Creators of the world (that's you!) who are looking for inspiring tools to live by and love by that add to the joy and meaning of life for self and others. ***In humble gratitude, Mary Mac***

Table of Contents

Introduction

Life has a way of showing you exactly what you need to see, just at the right moment. So one day, I find myself looking down upon a woman about my age, violently kicking, pounding her fists, wailing woefully into her pillow and writhing in agony.

"What on Earth is she carrying on about?" I ask myself, mystified. As she comes up for air, I hear a gentle yet imperious voice exclaim, "Just relax!!!"

My eyes dart randomly around the room, in search of the source of the voice, without success. It is a few moments later, as I rest my gaze back on the scene below that I realize, with intense interest that the woman on the bed............ is me.

"Holy Crap I am out of control!" I expound to myself. The voice repeats itself. "Just relax!"

Immediately I feel my scalp releasing its tenacious clench on my neck. The tears stop flowing. My face reshapes itself into human form. I feel like laughing. In fact now I am laughing!

"What just happened?" I wonder in the direction of the ceiling.

This wasn't the first time I have found myself in a fetid frenzy of elliptical emotion. I notice that it is weekdays, before school time, that have a tendency to begin blissfully and end in an eruption of evil!

As I walk my son introspectively to school, a magical phrase dances into my my mind. 'Cultivate the Morning Calm.' "Yes! That's just what I need to do! Cultivate the Morning Calm!" I'm not sure how, but I have a pretty good idea where to start........ "Just relax!"

This fun little book was born out of my desire to have a more serene and happy beginning to each day, a desire echoed by many of the people I have spoken to since deciding to explore this topic! I wanted to feel a sense of flow in the morning, a sense of harmony instead of the chaos which was the reality of my usual morning routine. I had been experiencing that *flow* in so many parts of my life already, but more often than not, I was finding myself tense, reactive and grouchy in the morning as I herded the kids out the door. A strong desire arose in me to figure out how to help myself achieve a calm, happy start to the day and to share that with others.

As a Health and Wellness Coach and HUMAN GENIUS CREATOR (as all humans are!), I know that I have the power to create whatever I decide I want in life and I also know that whatever I am living at the present moment I have also created! I take 100 percent responsibility for whatever manifests in my experience. So after looking objectively at my morning 'freak outs' I decided to admit that ***I*** was actually in control and do something about it.

I began observing others around me going about their mornings, at school, in traffic, at the supermarket. As I observed many families arriving at school, I often saw parents, red-faced, shouting commands to those powerful small humans who were grinning cheekily, happy that their button-pushing was paying off so well!

Sometimes the children were reflecting the anger of the parent and shouting back. I noticed that these displays of anger seemed to happen in and around the car, but as soon as the family was out of the car, the 'public image' seemed to shoot into gear and there was far more patience being practiced. (Yes I was being a little bit nosy but for a good cause!) And I could relate to this personally of course. I have far more patience under public scrutiny! Of course I did observe happy, relaxed interactions between children and their caregivers also! I just saw lots of room for improvement.

I thought about those without children to get ready in the morning and how many people experience stress just getting ready for work. They can't seem to get up in the morning, get up late, leave late, don't allow for traffic hang ups, worry about the day ahead. With or without children, everyone would benefit from a calmer, more serene, more focused and intentional start to the day!

The school drop off would be a time of joy and playfulness, not the stressful scuffle it seemed to be for many. And the roads would be such a pleasure to navigate if this calm should spread. The grocery line would be family time instead of threats and bribes time, which I'm sure would please everyone.

Doesn't it seem like the way you start your day is generally how you finish it? When you get out on the right side of the bed, so to speak, don't you just feel a flow to your day that you miss when you start the day in chaos?

Someone once told me that the best way to learn something is to teach it, which on the surface sounds a bit ridiculous, however I have felt and seen the truth in this statement. I would figure out how to have a calm and intentional start to my day and I would teach as I learned. And so this little book was born.

I began to apply this mind to what might help us all to be more happy and calm in the morning. First I examined myself to see what it was I was doing in the morning. I noticed that no matter how early I got up, as soon as it was close to leaving time, I'd begin to rush around, feeling stressed and speaking more harshly. Often my kids would be the ones to say, "Hey Mum! Stop freaking out!" And I'd immediately thank them and snap back to the moment. I had practiced the belief that the present moment was always perfect no matter what was happening...... if I remembered to be IN IT.

So what causes people to stress out? Is it some quality of the circumstance you find yourself in? If this was the case and everyone had a similar stress reaction to that particular situation, then we could conclude that the circumstance caused the stress. But most of us know at least one person that seems to stay unruffled in most situations. So I concluded it must be something people are doing with their minds. People are all different in the way they deal with feelings of stress or situations which may provoke stress because they do different things with their minds either consciously or unconsciously, mostly unconsciously!

Once I realized this, I finally understood what was happening to me in the morning. I had a flashback to high school and even primary school when I was getting ready in the morning. Every morning my friend Jill would come over and we'd walk to school together, but I'd always be in a flap getting ready to leave for school and putting my contact lenses in at the last minute. That is the memory Jill has of it too as she told me she remembers me rushing to put my contacts in after she arrived. I had had this rushing habit ever since then!! That's a lot of mental habit pattern.

It is our mental habit patterns that are running our lives in most cases. When we slow down and get intentional about our lives, we stop blindly reacting to things and have more control of our mental and emotional states. It's funny how easy it is to see what other people need to do to 'get it together,' yet I had missed this habit of mine for so long!

Through my coaching and my own self discovery journey, I have learned the power of my own conscious intention in life. The power to shape your life is largely influenced by what you 'intend' for your life. Most people have not thought about what they intend for themselves. You get to choose how you intend your life to unfold! You are not the subject of random uncontrollable circumstances as it may seem sometimes. If you unconsciously intend to hold a grudge against someone who has hurt you, you will create anger and resentment for yourself over and over until you decide to create something different for yourself. If you consciously intend to create peace within yourself and a calm morning routine, your creative Life Force energy gets directed toward creating that.

In the Cultivation of my Morning Calm, I decided to hold the intention to become aware of myself in a way that would allow me to unravel this cycle and free myself up to choose my reality instead of repeating old patterns. This book is the result of the application of mind to a question whose answer is passionately summoned. In other words if you really, really want to know something, the answer will find you! You have the ability to summon answers to whatever questions life offers you. You have access to Infinite Wisdom. This I know for sure and hopefully so will you by the time you finish reading.

This desire and intention to free myself and inspire others has led me to a metaphor that works so well for what I want to express here! In this book we are going to learn how to *Cultivate the Morning Calm* by learning the *Causes of Calm* and then lovingly planting a bountiful garden of peace and serenity by following nature's example.

If you want to grow a flourishing vegetable garden, what steps do you take? Planting your garden of calm looks very similar:

1 Prepare the Soil of the Mind
2 Sow Seeds of Calm
3 Cultivate your Copious Crop
4 Harvest your Fructicious Fruits
5 Celebrate Life in all its Juiciness!

In preparing the soil you will learn how to fertilize the garden bed of your mind by establishing **awareness of the moment** through meditation, developing an **attitude of non-judgment** of your experiences and **discovering the loving, wise being you really are**! This process will make your garden bed healthy so it can give your seeds the nutrition they need to grow...

You will learn to plant seeds, the fruit of which contain only the quality that you wish to reap, in this case, calm. The thoughts you choose to think throughout your day *are* the seeds you are planting, the seeds that will germinate and grow into your garden of life. Most people are not choosing their thoughts consciously. You are letting your past patterns of thought dictate to you what you will think. This process will be revealed to you and you will love your newfound control over your thought process.

Before the cultivation process begins you need to do a bit of self-examination to see what habitual thought patterns are going on in your mind. Then you will pluck out some of the old thoughts (weeds!) that have hindered your garden's growth in the past by replacing them with the kinds of thought-seeds that will blossom into little seedlings of calm and then into the juicy fruits you desire! Seeds of **appreciation** and **positive intention** are the kind you want. These are the biodynamic power seeds. The seeds of negativity will get weaker and weaker as you refuse to sow them and as they get crowded out by the seedlings you really want to grow!

During cultivation of your copious crop you will tend to your young calm seedlings with twice daily doses of food, water and sunshine, otherwise known as **meditation, appreciation** and **positive intention.** These are powerful fertilizers without which your morning calm cannot thrive.

Harvesting your fruits is a pleasure as you get to enjoy the results of your care and efforts in most every aspect of your life, not just the morning routine! You will look carefully at your life and find the changes you have been seeking beaming at you in the mirror and in the faces of those you love. You may also find some sour fruits that came from seeds you planted out of negative habits from the past. This serves you well. You then know what to work on for your next crop! You will share the sweet fruits of your harvest joyfully, knowing that whatever you choose to give is so well appreciated.

You'll learn the **Three R's** for the moments of the *uncalm* when you are experiencing strong moments of doubt or even anger, frustration or blaming others. You'll learn to Relax, Remind and Refocus in these moments to bring yourself back to the moment and what you intend for your day. Being gentle on yourself will help produce a more satisfying harvest.

After the harvest is the time to celebrate! You can look back on your newfound skills to create calm and appreciate all of the process; the fruits, definitely the fruits, but also the challenges and pain you may have experienced along the way! It is ALL growth! It is ALL what we're here for! It is ALL love.

When you can appreciate all aspects of your day, the good, the average and the not-so-pretty, you will be enjoying life the way it is intended to be enjoyed: AS IT IS. And you will also find that your life transforms before your very eyes, more and more closely resembling the life you've always known was possible.

I have studied the Laws of Nature from two powerful perspectives: The Law of Nature as taught by the Buddha and the Law of Attraction as taught by Abraham via the lovely Esther Hicks. I believe these are 2 perspectives that in essence express the same powerful message: 'As you sow, so shall you reap' or 'That which is like unto itself is drawn'.

Buddha's teachings show us that Nature's seeds contain certain qualities; the qualities of the fruits or tree or vegetable that is grown from it. Whatever the nature of the seeds will be the nature of the fruits. You will learn to select your seeds according to your intentions and plant your seeds with wisdom in the cultivation of your morning calm. The Noble Eightfold Path as taught by the Buddha is a powerful guide to achieving this and is outlined in Chapter 6.

Likewise, the Law of Attraction says that if you want to attract some thing or quality into your life you must offer thoughts of a similar vibration or feeling. Offer thoughts and feelings of love to attract love, thoughts and feelings of abundance to attract abundance etc. Same natural law, so powerful, so hopeful, so full of potential for all!

The OUTRAGEOUS JOY Journey is a book I published in 2009 and it speaks directly to and from that part of you that ***knows*** and shows you the process of summoning your own answers through your channel of Life by discovering your own Inner Voice. I will show you an exercise for connecting with and hearing your own Inner Voice in Chapter 4. If you are looking to do an in-depth study of yourself and delve into the big questions in life, *The OUTRAGEOUS JOY Journey* would be a great place to go after this! It is a project for people actively working on understanding all aspects of themselves and their physical, mental and spiritual intentions and purpose here in this reality.

This time, I wanted to write a book that was short enough not to be intimidating to busy people, but that would help you gain enough insight into life, self and the Universe that it was useful to all **Human Genius Creators** in discovering your own power to cultivate ANY positive aspect of life you choose for you.

Nature intended us to learn (re-learn) from her! The processes of nature can be witnessed everywhere and if you apply her principles to any aspect of life, you will find the wisdom you seek in that area. If you want a deeper understanding of body image or beauty, you will be shown how to use this metaphor to create that which you seek. If you want to understand your own abundance, follow the example of nature and create it! This garden metaphor for teaching and learning really works for me! Hope it does for you too! See you in the garden!

Chapter 1

The Causes of Calm

In order to cultivate this morning calm, I needed to look at the causes of calm in order to figure out how to do it. When I asked myself what has had the most calming effect on my life, the answer was obvious: **Awareness of the moment**, through the practice of *meditation.*

I have experimented with a few different forms of meditation through the years, but my current practice is particularly powerful in stimulating an awareness of the moment. I have been practicing meditation for 10 years using this technique which is specifically aimed at cultivating awareness of the moment. It is this meditation that you will use in the cultivation of your morning calm.

Awareness Of The Moment

The reason meditation helps so much in the creation of calm is that it gives you the *power of focus* and with the power of focus you can remember to be **aware of the moment.** Meditation is a technique that will strengthen the focusing ability of the 'monkey mind' which tends to jump from subject to subject like a monkey jumps from tree to tree. Meditation trains your mind to be more peaceful.

This moment is where all of the power of the Universe lies because when you are aware of *this* moment **as it is**, you have the power of **choice**! When you are aware of this moment, you have the space to think about and choose your next action instead of re-acting. You can choose where to focus the power of your Life Force in the creation of your life.

You can choose to focus your energy on rushing, on what people are doing that you do not like, thus bringing more of that to you via Law of Attraction or Nature, or alternatively, you can focus it on remaining calm and noticing what is happening that pleases you, thus bringing more of that your way. You can choose to focus on what you are dreading about your day or what excites you. Without awareness of the moment, however, you may well just blunder through the day controlled by your habits of thought and reaction.

When you are blundering through your moments focused on what happened in the past or what might happen in the future, you are living a life of reaction.... No power, no choice. The power to choose to be calm, or to love or to be or do anything can only be had by those with focused minds that are aware. The process of bringing the attention back to the breath in meditation is the process of gaining control of the mind, empowering you to choose where to focus. You'll learn this basic technique in Chapter 2.

Know Who You Really Are!

Cause number two of calm is, knowing Who You Really Are! For those of you who are unfamiliar with the *Teachings of Abraham* or have not read *The OUTRAGEOUS JOY Journey*, 'Who You Really Are' is another way of saying HUMAN GENIUS CREATOR!

Has anyone ever told you that you are a genius?? Do you believe that you are or could be? Do you believe there is an intelligence that created this world? I believe this intelligence is the Life Force itself and that if I am filled with Life Force as I must be in order to be alive, then it follows that I must be potentially as intelligent as The Force that created me.

This potential is realized when I let that Force inhabit me fully. And the extent to which the Life Force can inhabit me is dependent upon how I **choose** to see the world. When I choose to see the world and myself as purposeful, filled with love and abundance in insane quantities everywhere, then I am letting The Force flow freely and I have access to all of my answers. When I let myself dwell on thoughts of blame, injustice or scarcity, I deny myself the joy that is my natural state of being, and I restrict the flow of wisdom to me.

In his book *The Breakthrough Experience,* Dr. John Demartini told me that, "I am a genius and I apply my wisdom." He suggested readers should repeat this to themselves often until they believe it. I love playing these games and so I tried it, even out loud! I got a lot of entertainment from just watching the looks on people's faces when I announced I was a genius and I apply my wisdom!! But soon I began to see signs that this was true.

I acknowledged to myself when I had insights into people and life that I thought were quite rare and unique. And I found that the more I believed in my own genius the less I felt drawn to announcing it to the world. It was just a quiet knowing that I had this voice inside me that could tell me anything I could believe that I was capable of knowing.

What's so exciting about that statement is that as I begin to believe in the power of my own intelligence, I begin to believe that I AM capable of understanding the complexities of The Universe. At first I would only get answers to questions if I believed I could understand them. But now, I know I have access to much, much more! I only have to believe in my own genius or ability to let the genius in!

So, in order to cultivate your calm you have to believe that you are capable of doing so! Believe in your own genius and have faith that so long as you are alive, you are not alone... The Force is with you. (yeah, sorry 'bout that)

An Attitude of Non-Judgment

> A farmer had one old horse that he used for tilling his fields. One day the horse escaped into the hills and when all the farmer's neighbors heard about it, they sympathized with the old man over his bad luck. *"Bad luck? Good luck? Who knows?"* said the farmer.

> A week later, the horse returned with a herd of wild horses from the hills and this time the neighbors congratulated the farmer on his good luck. *"Good luck? Bad luck? Who knows?"* said the farmer.
>
> Then, when the farmer's son was attempting to tame one of the wild horses, he fell off its back and broke his leg. Everyone agreed that this was very bad luck. Not the farmer, who replied, *"Bad Luck? Good luck? Who knows?"*
>
> Some weeks later, the army marched into the village and forced every able-bodied young man to go fight in a bloody war. When they saw that the farmer's son had a broken leg, they let him stay. Everyone was very happy at the farmer's good luck. (reprinted from www.?

When you observe yourself and life *as it is* without reacting to it, just to see what comes up, you are approaching life without judgment. This is the third key to calm.

An **attitude of acceptance or non-judgment** is essential to anyone making strides on the path to calm. As soon as you judge your experience you create an emotional reaction within yourself. A judgment of 'good' creates a reaction of craving for more. In other words a feeling of negativity arises in you when that thing that is so 'good' is missing such as a lover or something precious you have lost. A judgment of 'bad' creates a reaction of aversion, anger, hatred, annoyance and you will act to rid yourself of the thing you think caused your negative feeling. If you can learn to simply be with your experience, whatever it looks like, without judging it, you will be very quickly achieving your calm.

A very powerful concept taught by Buddha is called *Anicca* in Pali language, the language spoken by The Buddha.

Anicca means, temporary or ever-changing, and is a perfect description for this experience of life we are having. Anicca will prove to be your devoted friend in developing this acceptance. When you realize that all things are changing constantly it is easier to let go of your attachment to things being a certain way in order for you to be happy.

Everything we can perceive with our senses, even our physical bodies, is arising and passing away millions of times per second, making *attachment* to anything in this physical world nothing but misery because it either leads to craving for more or aversion to what *is.* The thought of craving for a wanted thing or having things you judge as bad in your life evokes negative emotion. When you avoid judging your experience, you can allow your life to be whatever it is and be happy anyway. Remember Anicca and lighten up!

Is it possible that you can allow your morning to be whatever it looks like on the outside and yet remain calm on the inside? If you can, and that is what this book is aiming for, gradually the outer expression of your inner world will change and you will see the actual physical evidence in your morning routine. You must cultivate the calm first.

As you prepare the soil of your mind in the next chapter you will discover ways to train your mind to be ***aware of the moment,*** develop knowledge of ***Who You Really Are*** (your true nature) and develop the ***attitude of non-judgment*** that is so helpful to your own peace of mind.

A notebook will be very helpful for completing the exercises that will prepare your mind for the journey ahead. Some of the exercises you can simply do in the privacy of your own mind. Try to keep your insights all in one notebook so you can refresh your mind as to what you have discovered along the way. I'm so excited for you!! Actually I'm so excited for me too because I have just rounded a corner in my discovery of The Morning Calm and have been practicing three steps I just created that work so well in the moment of the *uncalm*. I am excited to share them with you in chapter 4!

Mary Mac

Chapter 2

Preparing the Soil

For any seed to take root and grow, the soil in which it is sown needs to be fertile. It cannot be full of grass and weeds which steal the nutrients from the seedlings of calm you are nurturing. But before you learn how to prepare the soil of your mind, I have some good news! Your desire to become calmer in your outlook and spread that calm to others in your environment means your soil has already begun to be prepared! You WANT this and when you have a genuine *desire* for something, you are in the perfect position not only to receive your answers, but to be willing to do the work to get there!

Children learn far more effectively when they first experience the desire to know something, and then are guided toward the information they seek rather than being shown how to do something they have not asked for. This is part of the philosophy of Steiner or Waldorf Education, which my son and I are exploring together presently. It's wonderful to hear him say, "Mum, I want to know how to read!"

At the Sudbury Valley School in the US, children are not taught anything unless they have asked to learn about it. This means that some children do not learn to read until they are 9 or 10 years old or older! But once their natural DESIRE to learn to read comes forth, these children learn to read quickly and catch up with other children their age within months!

When your desire to know something or do something or be something is great, you summon a tremendous amount of energy or Life Force through you to the creation of that thing. That's when you attract a book like this or things fall into place o provide you with something you have wanted or to help you make a change you have wanted in your life. The only thing that ever gets in the way of those things manifesting is your own doubts about yourself or the possibility of that happening for you.

Your **DESIRE**, whatever you really, really want, is Life's desire for you! You cannot separate you from your Life Force. And in my view, your Life Force IS God, it is Source, and it IS part of you. You are ready. You are here.

In preparing the soil of your mind you will do some self-examination of your present habitual thoughts about life and self and begin the creation of new habits of thought where required to enrich the soil of your mind. You will learn a technique of meditation to develop your power of focus in the present moment. You will perform an exercises to help you discover who you really are, how to appreciate yourself and how to let go of your judgments about yourself and the events of your life so that you can begin to remain calm in stress-provoking situations.

Your mental habit patterns, habitual thoughts and beliefs truly define your reality. For example, if you believe that you will be truly happy and complete when you have attracted the perfect partner into your life, this IS your reality. Every time you look at your life, you will see yourself as not complete or fulfilled or happy until partnered. You will live each day from a place of lack.

Now if you choose to believe that you are capable of deep happiness and fulfillment, partnered or not, you will act from this premise and so it will BE. You will see all of the ways you are happy and fulfilled and whether partnered or not, your life will be so much more abundant. The bonus here is that from this platform of abundance, your happiness will act to attract others to your life far more efficiently than in the first scenario where you were projecting an image and feeling of need or lack.

Your work is to begin to cultivate beliefs that are in alignment with the knowledge of your own 'wholeness' and absolute power in the creation of your life.

Examine Your Mind

What is the soil of your mind like presently? Is it richly nourished with optimism and feelings of wellbeing? Is it overcome with negativity and feelings of helplessness? Most of you are somewhere in between or may have a mixture of thoughts and feelings from moment to moment. I refer to 'feelings' because your feelings are a reflection of what you are thinking about and the judgments you make about those subjects.

Your feelings are feedback from your Inner Being or Life Force saying that what you are thinking is either in alignment with your intentions of your own wellbeing or not. Anytime you are feeling anything less than good, you know you have made a negative judgment about your experience of the past, present or future. Painful feelings mean that you are focused in a way that does not agree with what the wise part of you knows; All Is Well. You are judging your experience as bad when really it just IS.

"A belief is just a thought you keep thinking over and over." (Abraham) Most of your deep-rooted beliefs have come from something you heard over and over as a child, and continued to hear over and over in your own internal dialogue as an adult. If you had optimistic, happy caregivers you may have heard things like, "You always land on your feet don't you?!" "Things always work out in the end....." And you will see how that belief in the general goodness of the world is reflected in your own life today.

Or you may have grown up with, "Life is hard!" "We can't afford that!" "You can't do that! You'll fall and break your neck!" In the second scenario you learned that life is dangerous and you are not capable of handling it on your own. You may have heard your mother say to herself in the mirror, "How did I get so fat?? I need to lose weight! I am disgusting!" Well as a little girl, you would have assimilated that 'fat' mentality into your belief system, generalising that to yourself, even practicing that fat monologue in the mirror. The good news is that you can consciously choose new thoughts to feed yourself, thereby cultivating new beliefs about yourself and the world.

The way you consciously cultivate beliefs is by training your thoughts in the direction of what you *want* to believe and then FEELING your way through life to see how well you are assimilating them. When you feel good, you are thinking in the direction of wellbeing. When you feel bad, you are identifying with a past negative belief.

So a good place to start this process of examining the mind is to identify which thoughts you are habitually playing within your mind and how these thoughts are affecting you.

> **Self-Talk Exercise:** *Over the next week take the time to notice the types of thoughts that make up your running commentary on life, your operating system. When you notice a feeling of dissatisfaction or any sort of negativity, gently let yourself relive the moments preceding the feeling to see what you were thinking about yourself or another or a situation. Write this thought down. When you notice a feeling of happiness or peace wash over you, ask yourself what the thought was that preceded that feeling. Write it down. Specifically notice this talk in the morning. Do you say things like, "I'm always running late!!?"*
>
> *Don't judge yourself when you find you are thinking something that causes you to feel bad. Just try to detach and observe yourself like you were observing a cat going about its day. You wouldn't judge a cat for sleeping too long or stretching too much. You might find that you don't remember to notice your feelings or thoughts. That's ok too because the next section is*

dedicated to the technique that will help you become more aware.

Awareness Through Meditation

One thing that will definitely help bring you to an awareness of this moment is meditation. This is not a technique of visualization or going to a happy place in order to change how you are feeling. This is a technique to cultivate your awareness of this moment so that you can observe it objectively, As It Is. When you learn to observe your moments in this way, you can avoid making judgments that cause you and others to experience such dissatisfaction, anger or even depression at times. Here you will learn to meditate to cultivate your awareness that this is the moment of power and choice. You will begin to see how an attitude of non-judgment serves you well in your cultivation of calm.

Meditation Exercise: *You will need at least 15 minutes of uninterrupted time to learn to practice this meditation. Find a quiet place in which you feel comfortable and cozy. Sit on a cushion on the floor with legs crossed or alternately in a chair with two feet flat on the floor.*

Begin to notice the breath. Don't try to regulate the breath in any way. Just notice the in-breath and the out-breath. You may notice the breath is shallow or deep. It may be quick or slow, long or short. Your body may naturally pause in between breaths.....

After a few breaths you may notice your mind has wandered to a thought about something or another. Each time this happens, bring your attention back to the observation of the breath. It is the habitual tendency of the mind to wander. Observing this is part of the process of meditation. ***You are not trying to get your mind to be still.*** *This will be a natural product of the observation process!*

Continue to observe your breath noting the in and out breaths and refocusing your attention when the mind wanders for about 10 to 15 minutes. It is a good idea to set an alarm so that you do not open your eyes to watch the clock.

If a feeling of frustration or restlessness arises, remind yourself why you are doing this, to begin to train your mind to focus where YOU want it to be, namely, this moment. If the negativity persists, stop meditating and try again later, just for 5 minutes. Work up to 10 or 15.

A friend of mine found meditation to be very frustrating. She kept saying, "My mind keeps wandering away!! No matter what I do I can't stay with the breath." She said this with great heaviness and disappointment. This is not meditation.

You are just observing. If you think you have to *make* your mind stay with the breath, you will create resistance within yourself that does not serve you. Simply observe, as it is. Your breath goes in, your breath goes out again. Your mind wanders to this or that. You bring it back again and again observe the breath. Do not add any vocalization or visualization to this process

Do this exercise every day, once a day or more if you feel inspired, for the first week. In chapter 4 you'll see how we use it in the Cultivation of The Morning Calm. For now we are preparing the soil..... Meditation is a wonderful fertilizer!

Know Who You Really Are

Who are you? Who are you really? *What* are you exactly? What is this phenomenon you call 'I'? I feel it is important for you to answer this question for yourself so you are clear about what you believe. You may not know what you believe, but here is a great way of finding out! To start, it would be helpful for you to get out your notebook and answer these questions.

> **Who Am I Exercise**: *Ask yourself these questions.*
> *Who Am I?*
> *What Am I?*
> *Why Am I Here?*
> *What Is My Purpose Here?*
> *Just write whatever comes to mind. Then give your mind a rest for a minute, breathe, and ask again. See what else comes. Ask yourself now. Who are you anyway?? It does not matter what comes to mind here, just write it down in order to see the difference in your self understanding after practicing some of these techniques. The notebook is for your eyes only!*

What did you discover about yourself?

The point here is to get you familiar with thinking through these open ended questions. It is superb mental exercise. The point is not to get the right answer but to discover something new about you.

Now, because we are all one in essence, I am already familiar with who you are, at least in part. I want to tell you who I think you are because we all share that part of us called the Life Force, and so there are things we cannot help but share and know about each other.

I know you are a HUMAN GENIUS CREATOR just like me. I know that we share this thing I am calling Life Force and we are of the same energy that makes up The Universe. I know that all the wisdom of The Universe is available to you if you learn to tap into it or let it flow, or if you just stop doing whatever it is you do that stops the flow for you. When you doubt your capabilities or your worthiness you are resisting life. You are blocking your own energy flow; blocking your own wisdom. You feel blocked.

When you choose to believe in yourself and act as if you know you are worthy, capable and purposeful in your life, you feel wonderful! Life feels this alignment in you and brings you whatever you need to fulfill your purpose. I say 'need' because you may not necessarily get what you WANT at first. Like the song goes, "You can't always get what you want.........you get what you need!"

> **Self Appreciation Exercise:** *Use your notebook to make a list of all the ways you are capable or worthy, all the things you have achieved; all of the things you appreciate about yourself, physically, mentally or*

spiritually. Write down anything you have thought or anybody else has said about you that made you feel good.

These things make you feel good because they are true! Write until you are glowing with the knowing that you really are a gorgeous creature with the potential to do whatever you choose to believe you can! Maybe read that again to be sure it sinks in!

Try on the phrase, "I am a genius and I apply my wisdom." Just try saying it occasionally to yourself. It's fun!

Listen To Your Inner Voice

In order to know Who You Really Are, it is helpful to nurture your relationship with your own Life Force or Inner Perspective. You have your very own Inner Voice that will speak to you when you ask it to.

About 10 years ago I was in the painful position of deciding whether to end my relationship with the father of my two small children. So I took myself off to an island for the weekend to sort out my 'stuff'. I called it my self-discovery tour. I was walking in the National Park when I was suddenly overcome with grief. I looked up into the sky and cried, "WHO AM I???" To my shock and amazement I got an answer!

I heard, "You are a musician and a healer!!" The voice was like no other I've ever heard. It was absolutely unquestionable in its power and confidence. That statement was true, and no one would have disputed it. Then I was laughing and crying at the same time.

Since then I have discovered that it isn't only at times of great sadness that I hear my Inner Voice. I also hear it whenever I want to know something and my thoughts and feelings are in alignment with love. Because love is our natural state of being, when we are in the state of love-ing we are one with all parts of ourselves. We are one with wisdom, therefore we **know.**

Human beings are lovers. We need only to love to be truly happy. Nurturing the relationship with your Inner Being will help you to know this for yourself.

> **Inner Voice Exercise:** *After your 10-15 minutes of meditation think of a question you have been pondering. Write the question in your notebook. Then, wait, calmly observing what comes into your mind. If anything seems relevant, write it down. Those thoughts that are not relevant, ignore.*
>
> *You'll probably find that once you are onto a thought related to your question and you write it down, more and more thoughts will come to you on the subject. Keep writing until the natural flow of thoughts slows or stops. Reread what you have written.*

This process of letting your thoughts flow out of you onto the page is a very effective way of letting the Wisdom of the Universe come through you. Do you remember Tom Riddle's diary in the Harry Potter book The Chamber of Secrets? When Harry wrote in this diary, Tom Riddle could answer him from the nonphysical. This is how your diary can work for you! Sound spooky? Well it's not. It's totally natural. You've just forgotten about this part of who you are!

The question and answer diary process is how my relationship with Inner Perspective began to deepen. How did it work for you? You can also just lie down after meditation and ask yourself questions. Let your mind follow the thoughts that make sense and that follow the route of the question you have asked.

Meditation serves to calm the mind so you are offering less resistance or doubt than when you are simply observing what IS out in your world, which can lead to feelings of frustration (resistance). When you have just finished a meditation session, you are in a state of mind that is conducive to hearing your Inner Voice.

Even if you don't hear an actual audible voice or experience answers flowing through the end of your pen, your Inner Voice is speaking to you through your emotions. When you feel positive emotion, this is really your Inner Being telling you that what you are thinking about is in alignment with love and Who You Really Are. When you feel unpleasant emotions, this actually means you are thinking thoughts that do not gel with your Inner Being's knowledge of Who You Really Are (ie. Lover, Human Genius Creator, Worthy, Powerful, Capable). You are resisting life's flow. Pretty good feedback system, don't you think?

Your judgments create resistance in your being. Every time you negatively judge an event or feeling or person in your life, you create a resistance in your being that limits the flow of wisdom to an extent. So the key to transcending this resistance and allowing your own intuitive wisdom to manifest and blossom is to let go of your judgments!

Your emotions are constantly giving you important information about how you are directing your mind. Isn't it comforting to know your inner perspective is in constant contact and conversation with the physical you?

Good, Bad, Who Knows?

Lets look at the role of judgment in our cognition. According to The Buddha, there are 4 parts to the mind; the *cognizing* part, (or consciousness), the *recognizing* part, (or judgment maker), the *feeling* part and the *reacting* part. (Hart, William, 1987)

When information comes to us via the senses, the cognizing part of the mind alerts us. "Something is happening here!" The recognizing part of the mind which includes all of our past experience and emotional memory, kicks in and recognizes what the 'something' is and makes a judgment based on its knowledge of the past. "Is this thing bad or good?" If the judgment is good, the feeling part of the mind feels pleasure. If the judgment is bad it feels unpleasantness. Next a reaction occurs in the form of thoughts, words or actions that are congruent with the judgment made by the mind. The mind mostly does not even wait a moment to see if the judgment is correct or not! How often have you said or done something on the presumption that someone else had a bad intention only to be embarrassed when you find out you were wrong. Often in life, (and I only say 'often' because I try not to use the words 'always' and 'never', but really I mean always!) I have found that my painful experiences have led to something wonderful for me. I have also found that things or events I have judged to be good at one time, have had negative repercussions.

There is no good or bad, only perception. It is the way you think about things, the judgments you make which categorise things as good or bad and from these judgments, come reactions. The Buddha said, "In your seeing, there should be only seeing; in your hearing, nothing but hearing; in your smelling, tasting, touching, nothing but smelling, tasting, touching; in your cognizing, nothing but cognizing." Experiment with this idea.

Try eating something and just notice the nature of it without judging whether it tastes good or bad to you. Try it with all of your senses. Try thinking about someone you know. Imagine them if you can in your mind. Look at them. Observe their physical features, think about what things they've done, just from a detached place of observation. Notice if your mind begins to judge any of your observations and your resulting feelings in your body. Try again with another person or event.

If your intention is to have control of your mind and your moments and to cultivate a calm, loving and peaceful attitude in your life, it seems pretty important to limit the amount of negative judgment you dish out doesn't it? Luckily, the mind can be retrained to reflect any kind of attitude you wish to have. If you have the desire to be non-judgmental and the intention to be non-judgmental and an awareness of the moment your judgment arises, you've got full control of the moment. You see yourself judging, and have time to come back into balance before deciding what Action to take. Without this awareness, the judgment unbalances the mind and a Reaction occurs. It happens so quickly you do not even know it has happened because you were not aware in the moment the judgment arose.

At the moment you recognize that you have made a judgment and it is causing you misery, just hold that for a moment. Acknowledge it. Feel the feeling. Accept it. Then look objectively at it.

Say you are judging someone. Someone is being rude to you and you are reacting to it. Thoughts of how unjustified their rudeness is have come into your mind and you are feeling tense or angry. You are aware of what is happening. You know this is the moment of choice. You can choose to keep on this train of thought or you can choose to see it another way. You could say to yourself,

This person may be having a very bad day.
I don't know what may have happened to this person.
She is a human being just like me.
People are all different. It makes life interesting.
All perspectives are valuable.
She just wants to be happy too.

Choosing to do this in your moment of judgment is so powerful. You boost your own self-esteem by not taking her rudeness personally. This process will give you invaluable knowledge of your true infinite nature, and you will be reconditioning your mind to be less judgmental in the future.

> **Exercise in Non-Judgment:** *Think of something you know you are judgmental about and about which you would like to change your attitude. (ie. rudeness, lateness, sloppiness, selfishness!) Think about ways that you might actually exhibit the same quality. Write them down. If you don't think of any right away, just be with the question for a minute until some ways come to you.*
>
> *It is sometimes easier to be non-judgmental about yourself than another (or to deny your judgments of yourself!) because you think you have a reason to behave as you do. You justify the behavior to yourself. When you acknowledge to yourself the ways in which you are the same as the person you judge, it takes the charge or negative emotion out of it. You are less likely to judge that person or quality in the future and less likely to attract people with that quality in the future.*
>
> *Now think about ways of seeing that thing in a positive light. How does that thing serve the person who does it? Write down what comes to you. For example, I have learned to be grateful for the times when people have put me down or judged me negatively because those experiences caused me to rise up and discover my true goodness and potential, more so, I believe, than I would have otherwise.*

How is 'selfishness', for example, a positive thing? Well it could be seen as a positive thing for the person displaying this characteristic in that it allows her to do what she pleases, keep all her money to herself etc. It also allows others to take responsibility for themselves instead of relying on said 'selfish' person. And does it really matter so much what others choose? Let them choose it! Ultimately, when a person is in balance and understands who they really are they find a healthy balance of 'selfish' that includes service to both self and others. We are all selfish in many ways. How others deal with it is their own business! You can choose to waste your own energy on the 'faults' of others or direct your mind to healthier pursuits!

A Perceptual World

Ours is a perceptual world. This world only exists for you because you have the senses to experience it. All of your experience of life begins on the inside of you because you perceive this world through your senses and these feelings begin in the mind. All of the actions you direct outward originate with a mental action from inside your mind. If you accept this statement, then it follows that in order to make any changes outside of yourself, you need to make a change inside. This is what you have begun to do.

This world and, in fact, you, the physical representation of your energetic self, are temporary and changing every moment. We are taught in meditation practice to remember the temporary and transient nature of life every moment because when you know everything is temporary and changing you will find it easier not to be attached to the things or states of mind of this physical life. This in turn helps you to live in the moment and take each moment as it presents itself without requiring it to be a certain way in order for you to be happy.

In a perceptual or subjective world, what is the point of passing judgment? You can only judge according to your own perception, which makes your judgment only relevant to you! Yet we do it all the time! Remember the old adage that your judgments of others reflect more about yourself, your values, your life than they do about the people judged. This is quite true and not just in relation to others, but to life itself!

Your judgments are the only things that have the power to cause you misery. I try to see purpose in the things that evoke a negative reaction in me instead of judging them. (If you keep at it, you will find the meaning!))

If you decide to see purpose in everything that happens in the world regardless of what it looks like to you on the outside.... then presto, no misery, just meaning. This is the decision I made a couple of years ago now. I chose and every day choose to believe that we Humans as co- creators with Life itself, have a master plan, a grand scheme that we are all involved in and that we are all aware of on an energetic level. This is a subtle perception that only some humans are receiving presently. More and more of us are awakening, remembering our part in this plan, this creation, this beautiful growth process that we so brilliantly launched.

The body you inhabit is not solid but made of energy! Physicists now know that all things in the Universe including the body you inhabit are comprised of the tiniest of subatomic particles in motion. The Buddha described these particles 2500 years ago, well before modern physics evolved. These particles arise and pass away billions of times per second and are made up of the four elements, earth, air, fire and water. (Goenka, S.N.1987) In fact everything in this physical plane is composed of the same stuff. There is still debate about exactly what this 'stuff' is, but there is agreement that we are all one giant interconnected energy web of sorts.

We are *actually*, not just figuratively, all one. Your energy is radiant and is felt by every other part of the giant energy field! Isn't that exciting? It is a mistake to think of YOU as this body, separate from everyone and everything else. It is a mistake to be attached to any aspect of this existence to the point that it causes you pain. It is time to let go of the past, past judgments, patterns of behavior, anything that is not serving you in the here and now. Decide now who and what you want to be and act from this foundation. Let go of any negativity or grudges you may hold and give yourself the chance to begin again. This also frees others to do the same with their energy. Every moment offers you this opportunity.

Love Is All You Need ♪♫♫♪

You are here to love and to create. Often you think you just want to BE loved because it feels so good to have someone else's focus directed toward you lovingly, appreciating all of your wonderful qualities. Yes, that feels good, but it is ephemeral. Others cannot love you that way 24/7. When their focus changes, you may feel not so loveable! This is the illusion. Ultimately what you really want is not to be loved but simply to LOVE.

When you are in the state of love-ing you are not only loving whatever you are focused upon, but you are letting Life love you! This is the most sumptuous feeling that I have discovered in this life, and this feeling is 100% in your own control. It is not in the control of your lover, friends or family, for they will have their own focus and it will not always be you.

You have the power to choose to love, the greatest gift of all, and when you choose this focus under any circumstance, you are sharing that love with all of those around you. In fact, every other creature in the world benefits because of the energetic, vibrational nature of this Universe.

Knowing this, you are now ready to sow your seeds (thoughts, intentions) in the fertile soil of awareness, self-knowledge and acceptance (non-judgment). Choose your seeds carefully, for even when your soil is well prepared, if your seeds contain qualities that you do not want, you might grow weeds that stunt the growth of the calm plants you want to thrive! Chapter three will show you how to choose your seeds and plant them in the best possible conditions.

Chapter 3

Plant Your Seeds Of Calm

If you are an avid vegetable or fruit grower and you have prepared your soil, your next step would be to choose the seeds you wish to plant. If you want to grow mangoes, you will plant mango seeds. All of the qualities of a mango tree and fruit will exist within this seed, stored somehow within it, with the potential to create the juicy sweet mango. Now if you accidentally plant the seeds of a lemon, no matter how you nurture it during cultivation, you will never get a juicy sweet mango out of that seed.

In our metaphor, the seeds you plant are your thoughts and intentions. Now if you found you grew a lemon tree when you meant to grow mangoes, you might plead with Mother Nature, or bargain with her. You might say, "Please, please, give me mangoes! I want mangoes!! I will bow down to you and worship you everyday if you will give me sweet mangoes! And I deserve them!! I have worked so hard and I am such a good person!" But no matter how you argue, nature cannot give you the fruit you want if you have not planted the right seeds. Likewise, life cannot give you the calm or happiness you desire if you keep on planting seeds of negativity, irritation, blame, craving or aversion in your thoughts.

So how do you make sure to plant the right seeds?? You will ***feel*** it! You know fully well how you feel when you plant seeds of self-doubt, of jealousy, of rejection of others. How do you feel when you plant seeds of acceptance of yourself, seeds of love for others, seeds of appreciation, in other words? These are the seeds that have the qualities you desire. These are the seeds that will grow into the trees of life that bear the fruits you desire.

Plant Seeds Of Appreciation

In chapter two, you identified some of your self-talk; the habitual running dialogue you have with yourself about yourself, others and life in general. Now it's time to decide what habitual thoughts you'd like to keep and which ones do not serve you well. You can then replace those thoughts which cause you trouble with what you would *like* to be telling yourself and believing about yourself.

Many of you have listened to things that others have told us about ourselves when we were young, pleasant or unpleasant, and believed them. When we grew up, we picked up where they left off telling ourselves the same things. Perhaps you had a parent or sibling who told you that you were selfish or weak or no good at something etc. Eventually you grew up and moved out of the house, but did you take the messages with you?

> **Identify Your Seeds Exercise**: *Now is the perfect time for you to get out your notebook and look at some of your habitual thoughts. Make a new list of only the thoughts you feel serve you in your cultivation of calm……*
>
> *Now look at the ones that do not serve you and revise them to say what you would like to think about yourself or others or life itself. For example, if you habitually say to yourself, "I eat so much junk food, it's no wonder I feel so bad in the morning." You change that to say, "I feel so good when I eat healthy food and I feel so much better when I wake up." Do you see how that changes the focus subtly? The first is focused on the junk and feeling bad, the second focuses on health and feeling good. This is the habit you would like to create. So focus there. In the Appendix there is a list of the thoughts I used to change my beliefs. Perhaps they will help you formulate yours.*
>
> *If you used to say to yourself that you are always running late, think about a time that you were running on time! Acknowledge that to yourself and write down your new belief. "I can be on time! It sets my day up right and makes me feel organized." Make that your dominant thought about the subject. How powerful do you think it would be to be telling yourself everyday that you can handle anything that comes your way or that you're always in the right place at the right time?*

What do you ***want*** *to believe about you or others or life itself? What thoughts do you think would help you cultivate your calmness in the morning? What do you appreciate about your world?*

At first when you say these things to yourself you may feel a bit 'off' because they are not truth for you yet. Start to practice saying the thoughts on your list whenever it seems relevant. We'll use this list in the Cultivation Process in the next chapter.

I used to have a habitual thought that "I can't handle this!" in situations of conflict. So guess what? Whenever the going got tough, I'd freak out and either run away or throw a tantrum of some sort. I decided I wanted to be the kind of person who knew she could handle anything. This desire far preceded any belief I had that I could be this.

I knew that to create a belief you have to train your thoughts in that direction. And it was far easier than I expected because as soon as I found the *desire* for it, my attention was automatically sensitive to circumstances where I might usually react with "I can't handle this!" I found I could stop myself and say, "Yes, but what do you WANT? Oh yeah, I can handle anything!" And I found I could! And if I can do it, so can you. We are same. Human Genius Creator. No less.

Seeds of Intention

The other equally powerful type of seed you will plant are the seeds of your powerful, creative intentions for your life. There are many wonderful books out now on the power of declaring your intention to yourself and the Universe. Still, you need to **make intention setting a habit** in your life. To do this, you must practice doing it, a lot.

Announcing your intention to yourself is powerful because it is a way of projecting energy into the future. I believe that we are here to remember our own power of creation. That is what we do. We create. I don't know how or why we humans got to this place of unbelieving in our own power, but all the evidence suggests that NOW is the time all of the Forces are coming together for our reawakening. It's so exciting!! (See Gregg Braden in Recommended Reading)

Your intentions create. If I take the time to intend to be calm and aware in my morning routine, it makes a rather large difference to the *actual* goings on my household! Every time my rushing, panicking habit arises I acknowledge it and slow back down to awareness, I keep the calm vibe going on and because we all feel the vibration of others in our vicinity, I pass that on to the rest of the family. I *know* this is how it works because I have watched it happen over and over again.

Of course it works similarly when I get myself all worked up over something. The kids feel this vibe and reflect it right back at me in their attitudes and words. Do you have a similar experience? Have you ever thought about what you *intend* for your life? What you *intend* for your day? How you *intend* to be with your children, spouse, co-workers? Now's your chance.

Intention Exercise: *Apply your genius mind to the subject of what you intend for yourself, now or ever,* *just yourself or in your relationships with others.......*

In what ways do you intend to grow?
What are your intentions for your work or career?
How do you intend to feel?
Where do you intend to be in 5 years time?

Don't worry if you still have some doubts about the actual becoming of it. Just intend it.

Think about each aspect of your life that is important to you. Explore your intentions. Some areas to consider are: Health, family, friends, personal development, romance, fun and recreation, physical environment, career, money........

Write down your intentions in your notebook. Writing things down and reviewing them often, makes these things more active in your subconscious so you are more likely to remember them at crucial times.

When you intend something, you want to intend only things that you have direct control over, namely your own feelings, attitudes and actions. You don't want to intend for others to do things differently, because you do not control other people, not even your kids, especially not your kids!

Intention setting is the process through which I cultivated the belief that I can handle anything. I desired to be that way, I intended to be that way and I repeated the chosen belief that I could handle anything that came my way to myself. I reminded myself of this intention whenever I felt I couldn't handle something and that belief is the absolute truth for me now. I can handle anything that comes my way. I accept that there may be some pain associated with what life brings me, but I always know I can handle it.

What will be your truth? Intend it.

When To Plant Your Seeds

The conscious planting of seeds should be done when you are feeling good. After your meditation session in the morning is a good time to review your list of the new beliefs you are cultivating. During the day when you have a free moment and feel good, consciously choose one of your new thoughts/beliefs to reinforce. Say it to yourself and think of ways this belief is already true for you.

For example, say one of your new beliefs is that you are always in the right place at the right time. Think of a time when things just fell into place for you. Maybe it looked like you would be late for something and then you weren't or that you were delayed by traffic but as it turned out you got to your destination at exactly the right moment to receive some important information or experience, which you would have missed if you had been on time. Focus there until you feel the truth of your new thought that you are often in the right place at the right time. Best to avoid 'always' because it may make you remember times when the statement was not true and then you put energy into that! Once you believe the 'often' version, you can try the 'always' version which I have come to believe is true for me.

One belief I grew within myself is that, "I have the ability to bring out the best in people." I consciously grew that thought at times when I felt good, particularly on my walks in the National Park near my home. I used these magical walks to grow my new beliefs, concentrating on one thought and then being downloaded with ways in which this new belief was already true in my life and ways it would be true in the future. I found in those states of consciously focused joy, I could actually see and feel the future unfolding before my eyes as if it was already alive and happening.

Find time for enjoying nature, alone, and use this time to reinforce your new calm morning routine. Intend to plant seeds of the quality you desire to see in your life. Look for ways you are in control of your emotions, ways you see or bring out the strengths of others, ways that you remain calm and organized in the morning. Write them all down because your notebook will then become a place you can go for refuge, to see and reinforce to yourself how well you are doing!

The bulk of the information you will gain from this chapter will be from yourself, from your own experimenting with your own precious life, thoughts, feelings and intentions. Life is all about creating for yourself. No one else can create your life. No one else can do this important work for you. You deserve this care and attention you are giving yourself by being here now, examining yourself. You have done a wonderful job identifying what **thought-seeds** you wish to cultivate and understanding the importance of **appreciation** and **intention** in the planting process. It is certainly a valuable gift you are giving yourself and those you love.

In chapter 4 you will be given a routine for planting those seeds of calm intentions, but for now, plant them whenever you think of it!

As the fletcher whittles
And makes straight his arrows
So the Master directs
His straying thoughts.
Dhammapada

Mary Mac

Chapter 4

Cultivate Your Copious Crop of Calm

You have prepared your soil. You have carefully selected the seeds you would like to germinate and are beginning to plant them in your fertile soil. During the cultivation process you will develop a routine of care for your little calm seedlings. Once your seeds sprout, they need certain things to thrive. They need food, water and sunlight, otherwise known as *meditation*, *appreciation* and *intention*!

The human body needs food that is of the same nature as the body's chemistry. You need a balance of fruit, vegetables, proteins and starches that provide the same vitamins, minerals and other nutrients that are present in the cells of the body. When you consume lots of chemical additives with your food that are foreign to the human body, that is when you start to get into trouble. If the body cannot use these substances, it has to cope the best it can and try to eliminate them. This process largely depletes your energy supply.

Similarly, when you feed your mind toxic thoughts, you deplete or block the Life Force Energy you could be using to live this life! So you want to feed your garden with food of the same nature as your seeds, food your mind can use and that is nourishing for it.

The mind thrives on thoughts that are in alignment with the flow of life, namely thoughts of love, abundance, wisdom and knowing. You planted seeds of appreciation and positive intention and prepared the soil of the mind with meditation. So in your routine you'll give your thirsty seedlings twice-daily doses of the nutrition they need!

Twice Daily Feeding Exercise: *Your morning calm begins at night.*

NIGHT FEEDING

STEP 1: MEDITATION

Just before bed *is a good time to do your 10-15 minutes of* ***meditation*** *presuming you are not too sleepy. Try to get ready for bed before it gets to that point. After your meditation, sit or lie calmly and feel your body relax into your bed. Feel the softness and comfort around you.*

STEP 2: APPRECIATION.

Let your mind gently rest on the day you have just experienced with the intention of finding ***two things*** *you really appreciated and enjoyed about the day. Dwell on each of them for a minute, reliving the feelings of that point in time.*

After that, think of ***one person*** *you really appreciated that day and why. Let yourself feel the gratitude welling up inside of you. Smile ☺*

STEP 3: INTENTION.

Lastly, ***set forth your intention*** *to have a restful sleep, to let any conflict within you resolve itself in your dreams, and to awaken refreshed and ready for the new day's adventures. See yourself awakening with a smile, and the calm feeling of knowing that whatever happens, you can handle it.*

During step 2 if your mind falls upon someone or something that brings up a feeling of negativity, acknowledge that this too had meaning and purpose somehow, but do not inquire further. Move your attention quickly back to that which you appreciate. Say thank you for your whole day, for whatever happened was perfect for you and is leading you to where you want to be. Trust your life process. Trust yourself.

If you find it difficult to get to bed early enough to do the meditation and stay awake.... meditate earlier in the evening, but do the process of relaxation, appreciation and intention before you drift off to sleep. That is important for it sets the tone for your sleep and the manner in which you awaken.

MORNING FEEDING

STEP 1: MEDITATION

When you wake up *in the morning, do your morning 10-15 minutes of* ***meditation****. I find it even helps to* intend *that, meaning, state your intention to meditate with the awareness of the in-breath and the out-breath. If you are foggy first thing in the morning this intention will help you remember what you are supposed to be doing! Otherwise you risk just sitting there daydreaming or falling back to sleep.*

STEP 2: APPRECIATION

After meditation, let your mind find ***two things you love about your life.*** *These can be any two things that bring you into a happy place to think about. Rest there and enjoy that feeling for a minute.......*

At times you will feel agitated even after meditation and finding a place of appreciation may not be easy to achieve. Make a list in your journal at a time you are feeling extra special, of all of the things you appreciate about your life and why. Then during this step of the routine, if you feel agitated at all, get out your journal and remind yourself the things you appreciate about your life and read them all until you feel gratitude!

Now, think of ***one thing you are looking forward to today****, or appreciating about the day* *ahead. Feel how you will feel when you are enjoying those moments.*

STEP 3: INTENTION

Finally, ***set forth your intentions for your day****. Do you intend to be calm and in control of your emotions this morning? Do you intend to see what you love about others? Do you intend to be efficient and timely in getting out of the house?*

You create your own intentions. You may be specific as to how you want to be with certain people or in specific situations. Play around with setting intentions and you will soon find the style that suits you and feels most comfortable. Write them down if it helps. (It does!)

I still use an intention I learned from Abraham a few years ago. (See Abraham-Hicks in Recommended Reading)

'Today, no matter who I am with, what I am doing or what is happening around me, it is my dominant intent to look for that which I am wanting to see, or to look for that which makes me feel good.'

I then add that I intend to look for the good in all others and in myself, to spread the joy I feel and **to remain calm throughout my morning routine**! I intend to remain aware of my feelings and slow down when my habitual pattern to rush around arises. Establish this routine for yourself. I have found it so very worth the effort.

Now practically speaking, there are things you can do apart from the routine that will help you achieve your morning calm. You need to do some self-observation to see what is happening for you in the morning.

What are you doing with yourself din the morning? What disturbs you? Are you getting up too late to accomplish what you need to on time? Is it your kids taking too long or not getting up and ready? Are you worrying about what you have to do at work today? Do you find yourself getting worked up or angry?

The first step in changing these events is to change your outlook on them. If you are rushed because you are leaving too little time to get things done in the morning start by identifying your self talk around the issue of rushing.

You might be saying, "I'm always running late!!" and you beat yourself up over it. Time to stop that ball rolling. Think of a time you were up and organized on time. Say, "See! Sometimes I AM together in the morning!" How did you feel that day? Remember it, feel it. Would you like more of that?

Do you ever say, "I just can't get up in the morning!" Catch yourself and say, "Actually sometimes I feel great when I wake up. The more I continue on this journey of learning about myself, the better I feel and the more I feel like getting up in the morning. I love the feeling of having a bit more time to get ready and organize my thoughts about the day. And the more relaxed I am, the more happy and willing others around me will be to cooperate and have a calm and efficient start to the day."

If it's your kids not getting up and ready that bothers you, remember a time they were! Talk to yourself about that time. If you are not accustomed to talking to yourself, get used to it!! It is necessary in the process of retraining the mind to one with the qualities you desire.

The time to do this is not in the middle of an emotional reaction to something. Do this in a time of calm for you when you decide to **deliberately focus** on what you appreciate about your life, your children, yourself.

If you are getting up too late, obviously you can fix that. You will need to get up a bit earlier anyway to do your morning exercise. Plan to get up 20 minutes earlier than the first person normally wakes up in your household or earlier than you would need to get up for work. You may think you do not get enough sleep as it is BUT as you will be conserving your energy during the day by not being that emotional rollercoaster and by intending restful sleep the night before, you will feel rejuvenated.

Your morning calm can best be and really *only* be cultivated by giving yourself prep time. You will come to love this peaceful time of morning. It's worth it because you're worth it! And when you are filled with calm and peace, you are aligned with love and you share this energetically with those around you. When you are in conscious control of your emotional, energetic offering, you know you can affect the mood in any room and indeed the world! But let's stay in the room for now. We can talk about that later!!

It's when you are not in conscious control that you run into problems. You get yanked around by other people's negative 'vibes'. When others around you are expressing their negative thoughts and feelings, you will tend to feel what they are feeling because of our energetic, 'one' nature. You will then look for reasons why you feel that way, causing you to focus on whatever you are finding unacceptable about your experience!!

Most often you want to blame that other person for making you feel that way. In reality, no on can 'make' you feel anything, only *you* can. You control your feelings by choosing where to focus. Ever notice how some people tend to 'bring you down' while others have an uplifting effect? This can give you whiplash! The good news is that when you understand this process, you begin to exert conscious control of your focus. Increasingly you can choose how you want to react to the world around you and what you wish to offer in life!

Children are such wonderful teachers of this concept. How often do you hear a parent say, "You're driving me crazy!" In actuality, you are driving yourself crazy! Those little beings give you these gifts all the time, gifts of self knowledge, if only you would not react so quickly. Stop and ask yourself who is in control? Yes, it takes practice to be in control of your emotional state and consciously choose what you give out to those beautiful creatures. They are here to drive you crazy so that you finally figure out that it is up to YOU to stay sane! They do not have to change one iota. (What is an Iota anyway?? Better Google it!)

The Power of The Journal

It will be helpful for you to write in your journal about the process you are going through, what is working, what is challenging you, whatever is coming up for you as a result of this new thing you are doing. Change must happen if you do something different, something intended to help you experience your life more calmly, purposefully, lightheartedly. The saying goes, "If you always do what you've always done, you're always gonna get what you've always got!"

You are making important and powerful changes here and you will feel the effects. It will be interesting and inspiring for you to go back later and read your journal. Just write, if and when you feel inspired. Journaling is not for everyone, so don't pressure yourself or make 'work' for yourself. If it's not fun, don't do it. This is one of the key understandings you need to take to heart if you wish to transport your life to a more positive plane.

About two years ago, I began doing things purely for the joy of it. If there were things I knew I would be doing that I didn't think were fun previously, I tried a new way of looking at them. In other words I focused on what could possibly be fun or enjoyable in that experience ahead of time. And I found that I could really enjoy any situation I chose to bring fun to! Now I have trained myself so well that I find it nearly impossible to do anything I don't *want* to do. I either find a way to want to do it or I don't do it.

On the days that I succumb to the nagging of a child to do something I would prefer not to, and when I haven't managed to create the desire to do it in myself, I suffer severely in mental and physical energy for as long as it takes me to come back into alignment with myself. And this is completely dependent on how long it takes me to become aware of what I am doing and intend to do it differently! We humans are so fascinating!

When you use a journal you notice patterns and acknowledge points of interest along your path because you have the journal to refer to and use as a memory tool.

Most people cannot actually see a plant grow. And because you are with you every day, it may be hard to see yourself grow at first. The journal can help you to recognize your own growth because you can look back on where you *were* and see where you *are*. You can say, "Hey! Look what I've done! I am feeling so much better. I don't always get it right, but everyday I am getting more and more together in the morning and my family and I are beginning to enjoy our own company in the morning."

Other people who haven't seen you for a while will have no problem noticing your growth. It will be obvious. You will feel better, look healthier and be radiating a vibration of calm for all to feel!

Strategies For Moments of Negativity

We will always have moments of negativity until we become Saints or Buddhas. Accept this. For our purposes here it is helpful to entertain the belief that without the painful or uncomfortable times, we cannot experience the joyful ones. So we can develop a healthy respect for the times we feel less than radiant.

Do not denigrate yourself over the times when you are not in control and you say and do things you have not intended. There are forces working that are very powerful and you may be just beginning your journey into self-empowerment.

Sometimes it seems that others who are in a negative space have the power to bring you down. And sometimes you let them, accidentally. When this happens, in the next moment, begin again. This is what your daily exercises will do for you; give you the presence of mind to begin the next moment anew.

I call these negative feeling moments *balancing moments*, or **growing pains**! I can then see the purpose and productiveness of those moments of expansion.

The Three 'R's

Remember what the crazy lady in the introduction learned about the moment of The Un-Calm? As soon as she became aware of the moment she knew what to do! Your meditation practice is giving you the skill of awareness of the moment. This is exactly what you need in times when you feel anger or blame or out-of-control-ness arising!

If you are at the stage of awareness that you are sensitive enough to notice early on when you are feeling slight negativity, you have reached quite an advanced state of awareness. You probably have your own strategies for these times.

In the beginning, however, you may not remember to be aware of how you are feeling in the moment at all. It may take a more painful level of negativity to bring you to awareness.

When slight negativity has escalated to 'The Flap' (ie. Chicken with her head cut off) or 'The Witch' (Ogre for a male??), you want to remember the Three 'R's. The Three 'R's can save you from multifarious mental mishaps such as calling your mother in law a nasty name or telling your children you are never, never, never, never, never, EVER going to buy them icecream again! Why would you do that to yourself?? "Just relax!"

> ***RELAX:*** *Withdraw your mind from the situation and bring your focus into your body.* ***Relax your muscles*** *and take a long slow breath.* ***Accept*** *that you have just had a balancing moment. That's normal! Notice your breath going in and out once or twice. This will hardly take any time at all. Relaxing lets the tension or resistance out of you. It lets your energy flow more freely towards what you want.*
>
> ***REMIND:*** *Remind yourself what you want. What were the intentions you set forth this morning after your meditation? When you* ***remind yourself of your intentions*** *you automatically draw your attention to the positive and the negativity fades away and is replaced with a better feeling vibration. Your energy is now powerfully creating what you intended earlier in the day.*
>
> ***REFOCUS:*** *You should have a more pleasant feeling flowing through you now. This, more loving frequency is felt by all those around you. Once again you are clear about what you want. Now you can* ***refocus on the present*** *tasks at hand, bringing to them the vibration of calm. If you immediately return to the fluster, repeat all three steps. YOU CAN DO IT!*

At first, you may have to go through this process many times in a morning but not to worry! You are so wise! Soon you learn that you may as well stay calm because no amount of flapping or yelling or bribing or punishing is going to make your morning flow any better. Taking the time to be intentional about your thoughts, feelings and actions will.

Remember that when you intend something, it's helpful to focus on what **you** are bringing to the day or to this life. If your intention is for your kids to get out the door on time, you will experience an amount of doubt or resistance about this as it is ultimately out of your control. Or if you intend for your kids to get along and not fight with each other it's the same story. What you can control is how you feel and how you respond to the situations which are presented to you. Showing your kids that you are emotionally upset because they will not conform to your plans or your rules is just an unconscious game of power and you cannot win! Leave that strategy behind. If, despite your calm assistance and guidance they are still late, don't ruin everyone's day, yours included, by becoming angry and threatening. Let it go. Find something positive to say or just smile!

Spend time consciously intending to bring calm and joy to the morning, focusing your loving vibration on your children before they wake up or anytime you have the presence of mind to focus there. It is no joke that they will feel this offering from you and respond similarly. Kids are absolute mirrors for you. You give them anger, they will show you your anger with their own little faces. If you have the awareness of your moment and you can stop, mid-shout, and smile, they will mirror that to you and everyone will have a better time!

You can also intend something as general as flowing through the morning or through traffic or through life. Sometimes general intentions are better than specific ones because they are more believable and so feel more achievable when you focus upon them. Your intentions should feel like fresh air and sunshine to you when you make them! If they don't, you are probably intending something too far outside the scope of your belief. You doubt your own ability to achieve this intention, therefore you experience negativity. Try a different intention or a more general one, one that resonates with your heart.

Just because you are now intentionally creating your morning calm does not mean that your kids will be! They are limited by their own patterns and reactions. Your kids or partner may present to you many different vibrations in the morning, but since you have prepared yourself, you have the power to remain solidly in your 'calm' despite what is going on around you. You will not be yanked around by their vibes. In time, they will be uplifted to yours! Do *not* judge yourself or your progress by other people's morning attitudes or behavior. How YOU FEEL is your only yardstick!

The Buddha's word for this feeling of 'calm' we are striving for is 'upekkha' in Pali language or 'equanimity.' Equanimity is the willingness to be with whatever your life IS in this moment, without attachment. Equanimity is a state of nonjudgment which also includes an understanding of the temporary and changing nature of reality.

If you can step outside yourself and just observe life around you for a few minutes, you can have an inner dialogue something like this: "Wow she is really being aggressive toward me, hmmm." Or, "Oh look, my partner is trying to get me to agree to something I don't want to do! That's pretty funny. Can't control others can you!" Even, "I feel a little angry. I am reacting to the world instead of accepting or creating it."

You can go within and just examine this thing you call I, as an objective observer. This is what non-attachment is. Just observe your world as it is, without emotional charges or baggage or the need for things or people to be a certain way for you to be happy. Aren't you fascinating?!

You have created so much good stuff for yourself in this chapter! You have begun cultivating your Morning Calm by feeding your seedlings twice a day with Meditation, Appreciation and Intention. Well done. You have learned about the potential importance of Journaling for reinforcing all of the good you are doing yourself and all of the growth you are experiencing.

You have gained skills in The Three R's for use when the calm is nowhere to be found! RELAX yourself, REMIND yourself what you want, remind yourself of your intentions and REFOCUS your energy into the moment. Re-introduce the calm energy to whomever and whatever you were doing moments before. Be the calm. Your calm is not reliant on any external factor in your life. Only you have the power. In fact, your ARE the power. Believe in you!

Mary Mac

Chapter 5

Harvest Your Fructicious Fruits

Once you have intentionally planted your first crop, your awareness of your harvest will be continuous! I say 'intentionally' because you have been planting seeds all along! Every thought you have ever generated about yourself or life in general has been planted in your garden of life and has provided you with a plethora of interesting life experiences. Some you have enjoyed, others have been extremely unpleasant. You may not have realized how powerful those seeds were and how important it is to your wellness and happiness to be selective about the seeds you plant and to plant them consciously, with intention and love.

Whatever you are experiencing in your life is your harvest. You can tell by the fruit you are receiving whether you are planting purely the seeds of the fruits you desire or if a few seeds of negativity are getting in there! What is the nature of the fruit you are receiving? Is it sweet and juicy? Is it sour or bitter? Does it make you pull faces when you eat it?? For most it is a bit of both, because you are offering both sweet and sour words, thoughts and deeds in your life. That is the Law of Nature. As you sow so shall you reap. That which is like unto itself is drawn.

Also, some of the fruits that are ripening for you are the result of seeds you planted in the past. You may not have known that you were planting seeds with your thoughts and so you were not careful about the types of seeds you planted. A certain amount of your harvest will be a result of this, but gradually over time, the sour fruits of the past will exhaust themselves as their seeds fail to be sown again.

It took you all your life to develop the patterns of thinking that you now have. It may take more than one crop to retrain your mind! So you have some bitter fruits, some annoying or frustrating experiences. So what? They are there to learn from. They are indicators of what you are offering to life, as are the sweet fruits you love! Now you can thank those fruits for showing you where you can improve your mind.

Over time, your healthy, plentiful harvests will become more and more abundant. Your poor crops will be less noticeable.

Some Seeds Germinate Quickly, Some Take Longer!

Sometimes trees take awhile to produce edible fruit! That's OK because you have planted many seeds that will fruit quickly. Any seed of appreciation will fruit almost immediately if the appreciation has been deeply felt. You will see the results in the way your day takes shape, the behavior of others towards you, but most importantly, you will observe the results in the way that you FEEL.

Things or situations that felt bad previously, suddenly look good or are at least more tolerable because you have planted a seed of appreciation about that thing or life in general. For example, I was working at a childcare centre I had never worked at before and I was working with a carer who was not being very care-ing by my own judgment. She was very gruff with a little 18 month old girl and I formed an aversion to working with her because of it.

Now I know that I create my reality. I was bringing out, seeing or attracting this side of my co-worker by my own judgments of how I believed things 'should' be. This judgment was active in me and so that is what I observed. So I decided not to run away, and the next time i was to work with her I decided to change my outlook. I spent 20 minutes thinking about things to appreciate about her......how she *thinks* she is doing the right thing by these kids, how she has lived a lot of life already and hasn't really worked out how to be happy yet, how I did observe her being very playful and loving to one of the children....etc.

When I went to work later that day, I looked for that woman and I couldn't find her! She was there all right, but she was behaving totally differently. I had to ask myself if it was the same woman. I had only worked there two or three times so I thought perhaps it was someone different. But she had the same name!

By all means be specific with your appreciation as I did and if that helps you. Make it your intention (if it feels right to you) to find something to appreciate about everyone or everything that happens in your day. Sometimes I feel appreciation for a traffic jam because I know it is allowing me to arrive at my destination at the perfect moment for me. May not be on time, but perfect nonetheless. It also gives me the opportunity to practice 'equanimity.' Remember equanimity is the calm you experience when you are aware of the moment and not reacting to what is going on around you. You are of course taking 'action', but not 'reacting' emotionally.

> *Equanimity is the willingness to be with whatever your life IS, minus your judgments about it, minus your need to struggle to change it.*

If you are stuck in traffic (physically or mentally!) or pecking around the kitchen suddenly becomes 'the flap' or the 'chick with its head cut off,' remember the three R's. **Relax** for a second. Remind yourself this is an uncontrollable circumstance (traffic or other people!) and consciously choose your next thought. **Remind** yourself what you want. Something along the lines of 'to be calm throughout my morning' or to 'go with the flow' or to 'trust that things always work out in the end.' **Refocus** on what you were doing.

You must learn to ***Feel* for your harvest**. If you only look for it with your eyes, you will miss the most important changes. Things do not change from the outside to make you feel better inside. Change occurs on the inside first and the world follows suit.

Sometimes you get an off crop, one that fails to fruit for some reason or produces fruit that is inedible! Perhaps you had a rough patch and forgot to feed or water your crop. So be it. Begin again.

There Is Balance In Nature

In order to have anything to experience as 'positive' or pleasant, the opposite must exist. Without this contrast there is absolutely nothing to feel! I notice when I run my hand under warm water that if I adjust the temperature to exactly match my body temperature, I cannot feel my hand! Think about that for a minute.

If you didn't have a contrast between the temp of the air and your body, you would have trouble distinguishing your body at all if you sat very still. It is fun to meditate in the tropics where the temp is sometimes body temperature and humid like the body. There is very little to feel on a gross level except the beating of your heart and the thoughts upon the mind.

Likewise, if you didn't have contrast between what you want and what you've got, you'd be liberated in the Buddhist sense. Think about that for a minute. If there was no contrast between what you want and what you've got, ever, then you'd be in perfect balance wouldn't you? You would have no emotions because you would be judging nothing and so everything would be acceptable...... Would you still be here? Hmmmmm. If you want enlightenment, make peace with what is. Just some food for thought.

For now!.........If you want to keep harvesting the good stuff, (Stuff that feels good......It's **ALL** good stuff!), you will need to keep your soil prepared and your seeds of appreciation and positive intention on hand. With each cycle, if you keep returning the nutrients to the soil and you keep developing new fertilizers to enrich and feed your crop even more fully, the fruits will be plumper, juicier, sweeter and more succulent.

In other words, keep up your daily routines of meditation, appreciation and intention. Find buzz words that you can use to snap yourself back to the moment. In a coaching session yesterday, my client realized the simple word 'trust' was what she needed to remind herself to let go of a negative pattern of thinking she was carrying. This one word returns nutrients to the soil of her mind. Find words or statements that serve you and nurture yourself with them often. This will keep your soil at the proper PH or balance.

Keep weeding your garden! Like any garden, the weeds will continue to come so long as there are still roots left from which to sprout or so long as weedy thoughts keep getting put in the soil. The roots will eventually die out, even the deeply rooted ones and if you REALLY want to experience this go and do Vipassana!

Your awareness will allow you to see when you have planted a weed. Just replace that thought with one that is in alignment with your intentions; to be calm, in control, aware, loving, happy.... Don't worry about the negative thought you planted because those weeds need plenty of feeding on more and more negativity in order to flourish. Just accept what happened, and use the power of Anicca to begin again the next moment.

Before you were so aware of what was happening in your mind you may have let yourself roll in negativity for hours or even days giving lots and lots of food to those weeds. Now you know better. Don't think about the weeds; they are history. Just concentrate on what you WANT to grow. Don't dwell on what is done, create your next moment now.

Nature WILL provide for you if you work within its laws, the laws of nature. You reap what you sow. Keep your mind prepared and full of nutrients with daily and nightly meditation and sow seeds which will bear fruit that is sweet; those of appreciation, calmness, knowingness, wisdom, loving kindness.

Some Patterns Are Tough to Break

If there is a part of your life where you feel stuck, like you just can't seem to shift a negative thought pattern, have a look at it. Are you feeling particularly angry with someone? Why? What is he/she representing or reflecting for you? Your entire world exists as a mirror to tell you what you are doing with your energy. It is a representation of the energetic you. I figured out recently that my daughter was representing to me my own 15 year-old-self with all of the same issues I experienced when I was her age. I suddenly understood this, after struggling with her behavior and the feelings she brought up in me for so long. I was then able to acknowledge this reflection and to go back energetically and talk to the 15 year old me! I now see her experience as perfect for her, as mine was for me.

Is money a source of strife for you? Well what does money represent to you? For me money represents value. To some people money represents security or respect or any number of other things. For me it is value and I have recently discovered that what money symbolizes for me is my own self-worth!

Look at what money is symbolic of in your life. What you really want is not the money it is the *feeling* that having money represents to you. The feeling of security or self-respect, value or abundance is what you seek. So instead of constantly seeking the dollars in order to feel how you want to feel, seek that feeling. How are you already secure, respected, valued and abundant? What can you do to discover these qualities in yourself?

What we seek is always an internal experience. We have just been looking outside ourselves to find it! Silly us. I can't tell you the size of the chip that fell off my shoulder when I realized my money issue was about self-worth! I simply said, "Well how valuable am I??!!" Infinitely, of course. And I felt it through and through. I had spent a good part of my life feeling not worthy. I did not value myself highly. This pattern of thought was deeply rooted. That's why the subject of money is such an important instigator of growth for me!

The point is that some of these new seeds you are planting may take a long time to fruit for you depending on how deeply rooted the negative thought pattern is, but the more you can relax about it, the more quickly you will see the fruit you desire. Most people who have grown up without much money or with parents who showed high levels of stress and rushing or panicking, will have a fair bit of conditioning around the subject. So if one of your seeds is to become a millionaire, you just have to keep working at the source of the lack, your own conditioned mind and whatever money represents to you.

If your seed is planted with the intention of growing the morning calm, and your past conditioning goes very deep (you have practiced 'frantic' for most of your life), it may take a longer time to cultivate than if you have had some calm experiences as well. Ask yourself questions.

Is your health your biggest 'issue' at the moment? Do you ask yourself, "Why do I always get sick?" My own journey through this subject is quite interesting. I asked myself, "What does physical health represent to me? Well if I am healthy all the time, I am *responsible* for myself, I look after myself, I know when to say no and stay home and rest. It takes a lot of confidence to be healthy! And it is a big responsibility. No wonder perfect health is hard to come by.

To me sickness represented having a rest. I would get to go to bed and no one could argue that I didn't have a right to do that. Sickness served me well. But you know, after awhile I just said, "You know what? I don't really get to have a rest, anyway! Either my husband gets 'sicker' than me so I still have to do all the work, or I pressure myself to go to work or fulfill all of my 'responsibilities' anyway. Enough! I want health!"

Being healthy means being responsible for myself. I take full responsibility for everything that happens in my life and it feels wonderful!! I highly recommend it. And I feel healthier and stronger than at any other time of my life and

I'm 45. Sometimes I just have a guilt-free day in bed, just because I want to. Who's to judge? If I don't judge myself, no one else does either!

Taking a good look at the areas of your life where you experience particular negativities can be so helpful in creating a more productive garden! When you are feeling pretty peaceful, just gently ask yourself what gets in your way sometimes? What issues are relevant?

I find that what I *think* is the issue is usually just masquerading as the issue and the actual issue is underneath, lying in the subconscious. If I think others are not listening to me and it's a problem for me, the real issue is probably that I am not listening to myself! If I'm having a problem with other people being messy and leaving their 'junk' all over the house, the actual issue for me is probably that I am feeling really messy and untidy with my thoughts or am filling my thoughts with 'junk'. All of your experiences are important. They are all communication to you from within about what you are doing with your energy. This I know for sure. It's all good.

Learning from the part of the harvest that doesn't look so good, the crops that do not thrive etc, is just as important as appreciating the ways you are achieving the bountiful pleasures of life. Take note when things that seem negative turn out positive, because that can help you see more of your harvest as good, beneficial, growth producing and ultimately good for you.

There Are These Two Things

Remember the 'Inner Voice' I talked about early on? Well I had a wonderful conversation with mine one day. It told me two things that I believe are the key to creating absolutely anything in your life, especially the sense of calm you are seeking. This particular day, I was preparing for an interview for *'The Difference'* movie, an amazing movie being created presently. The theme of the interview was to be how I was hoping to make a difference to the world by Opening Humanity's Heart. So I did a bit of meditation and asked my Inner Being what it would like to tell the world in this interview. The voice said 2 things.

"Know Thyself" and "Love Thyself." And then I received the knowledge of why these were the only two things that you need to do to become Who You Really Are, to discover your true nature and to have access to the infinite wisdom of the Universe. Here are the words that came out in a song later that week.

These Two Things

We all come to a point in our lives when we ask,
"What's it all about?
You're sure you know there's something more
It makes you scream and shout
So close your eyes and go inside,
Ask yourself what you want to know.
Stay there and breathe so quietly,
Find the voice within.

There are two things that I've been told

By The Voice that knows.
They will take us to the place we know,
From where all life flows.
Just two little things are the key for all humanity,
To come into the light and do what feels right,
Trust the Voice Within.

These two things are so simple.
These two things will delight.
These two things may not be easy,
But they are the key to your flight.

Listen carefully.

You've got to ***know yourself***
To break the illusion that we're separate entities.
And you've got to ***love yourself***
And you'll love all others in this whole reality.
So grow compassion in your heart
Especially for yourself
Come into the light and do what feels right
Trust the voice within.

These two things are so simple.
These two things will delight.
These two things may not be easy
But they are the key to your flight.
Know Thyself
Love Thyself
Mary Mac

Perhaps you got that. Perhaps some of you need clarification. The reason that by knowing yourself you break the illusion that we are separate entities is that by examining yourself on subtler and subtler levels you come to the observation that your energy is constantly arising and passing away, in a constant flow between physical and nonphysical. The boundaries of these bodies that we perceive as separate actually do not exist. We are, in fact, interconnected. Now if we are actually interconnected, what is the result of loving yourself? You love all others simultaneously.

But, what is it to love yourself? I think loving yourself is first of all, accepting yourself AS IS. Could you be a 'better' person? We all could. But you are pretty fine just as you are too right? Yeah, you make mistakes. Sometimes, even if you *intend to love* over and over again, you will still have a reaction of anger, violence or other negativity that leaves you feeling sad, guilty or whatever your own personal form of punishment is for yourself. That's part of being human!

If we didn't have STUFF, we wouldn't be here. We're here to learn from the stuff. In fact, I'd go so far as to say we created this reality in order to create stuff to learn from, grow from and expand from! But that's perhaps the theme of another book.

Be Good To Yourself

My message here is for you to be gentle with yourself. Don't judge yourself so harshly, especially regarding your children. You are doing the best you can with what you've got and what you know right? Well now you've got more!

One thing I have learned as I've progressed from someone who thought she was never going to be good enough to someone who knows deeply her own self-worth, is that I am always doing better than I think I am! You often judge yourself more harshly than anyone else. Tell yourself,

"I am always doing better than I think I am!" And,
"My best just keeps getting better and better!"

And in those moments you feel you are doing really well, remind yourself, "I am always doing better than I think I am.......So WOW, I must be doing really, really well!" And you are.

Find things to praise about yourself and others. It feels so good. Praising others actually rewards you with pleasurable feelings because you feel their pleasure when they receive your praise! Praising yourself sometimes feels awkward at first, but get used to it! You will not become full of yourself and egotistical. Most egotism is just a mask for poor self-esteem anyway. When you have genuine respect for yourself and value yourself, you are naturally more humble and do not feel the need to talk up your successes.

Right now, go and look in the mirror and say, "I love you! I really love you, (your name)!" See what comes up for you. I dare you. Go on! The more you can love yourself the greater the harvest you will receive from this grand garden you have created here. When you love yourself you fill the well with love for the others in your life! The more you love you, the deeper and fuller the well will be. Remember the Law: As you sow so shall you reap.

But whoever follows the law
Is joyful here and joyful there.
In both worlds he rejoices
And how greatly
When he sees the good he has done.
For great is the harvest in this world,
And greater still in the next.
The Buddha

LIFE IS WHAT IT IS..... BE WITH IT, AND YOU SEE THERE IS ABSOLUTELY NOTHING MISSING FROM THIS MOMENT.....

Some quotes from the 'Tao Te Ching' Lao Tzu
translated by **John H. McDonald**

Since the beginning of time,
The Tao has always existed.
It is beyond existing and not existing.
How do I know where creation comes from?
I look inside myself and see it.
(21)`

If you want to become whole,
first let yourself become broken.
If you want to become straight,

first let yourself become twisted.
If you want to become full,
first let yourself become empty.
If you want to become new,
first let yourself become old..........
(22)

If you give evil nothing to oppose,
then virtue will return by itself.
(60)

The Master..........learns by unlearning,
Thus she is able to understand all things.
This gives her the ability to help all of creation.
(64)

Chapter 6

Celebrate Life In All Its Juiciness

What a beautiful job you have done here! I know it is beautiful because you were inspired to make the effort to read this book, to ask yourself what you want and to believe in yourself and Life enough to make a change. Are you celebrating your achievements? Are you rewarding yourself and your loved ones with intentional calm and joy in your day? Are you beginning to see how the so-called negative experiences of life can be just as valuable as the fun ones? I try to look at the unpleasant moments as the juiciest morsels that allow me to grow, to observe my own growth and to become who I really want to be and understand who I am at the ultimate level.

Actually I don't know anyone who has created large change for themselves and is now enjoying a fulfilling, abundant, loving existence who has not had to overcome adversity, most of the time extreme. They have had to let go of the past, forgive themselves and others and choose to see purpose in the events of their lives. They have chosen growth, as you are now actively choosing to look at yourself, nurture yourself, be brave and face your 'stuff' in order to grow and change as you intend. Commend yourself for the efforts you are making! You are one of the unique individuals who knows your own strength and power of creation and who understands the nature of 'reality'.

One can only come to this knowledge through self-observation: detached, self-observation. The most powerful path that I have found to date for training myself to observe this body/mind phenomenon objectively, which means unemotionally, non-reactively, scientifically, is the Path taught by Gotama The Buddha. I thought you might be interested in knowing the basics of this path in case it calls to you personally!

THE NOBLE EIGHTFOLD PATH

I would like to introduce you to The Noble Eightfold Path, if you are not already familiar with it, because it has been such a wonderful journey for me and some of you might resonate with it too. I feel that knowledge of this path can help you cultivate your morning calm and greatly add to your harvest!

There are 4 noble truths

The Buddha taught that there are 4 Noble Truths that anyone seeking enlightenment needs to learn.

1. ***The Truth of Suffering:*** You must accept that suffering exists. You can observe it with your senses, feel it with your feelings. It exists in this physical time-space reality we are presently living in.

2. ***The Truth of the Arising of Suffering:*** There was a beginning to this suffering. Suffering has an origin, a cause and that cause is craving caused by ignorance. Once you begin observing yourself it is quickly apparent that you are constantly reacting to one sensation or another on the body. Things that feel good you crave more of and things that feel bad you crave to be rid of. This is suffering.

3. ***The Truth of the Cessation of Suffering:*** There is a way to eradicate suffering. It begins with the point of contact of consciousness with the senses. This point causes the creation of sensations. Instead of reacting to the sensations, you learn to observe them equanimously. If you can learn to observe sensation in this way, you can break this link and eradicate misery.

4. ***The Truth of the Path Leading to the Cessation of Suffering:***

The Noble Eightfold Path is divided into three sections. You begin by practicing *Sila,* or living a moral life. You abstain from actions that harm self or others.

Samadhi is developing mastery over the mind, or concentrating the mind, which you achieve through the practice of *Anapana* meditation, the technique you have learned. Concentration of the mind on the breath leads to an awareness of each passing moment. Awareness of the moment allows you power of focus. When the mind strays, as is its nature, you bring it back to the breath or the present moment, which is where you live. Your power is in the present moment. Samadhi helps you remember that.

And if you want to observe yourself it will not help to concentrate the mind on an object outside of yourself. This is why The Buddha chose the respiration as the point of focus. It is a part of you and all others in this form, and it can be both conscious and unconscious. The breath is your bridge to subtler truths about yourself.

Panna is the wisdom you gain from the purification of the mind and it is achieved by the practice of Vipassana Meditation.

Within Sila are three of the steps on the path.

i. ***Right speech:*** Abstaining from lying, slander and backbiting, abstaining from harsh words and from frivolous talk or gossip. What you speak is very important in creation. Abstaining from the above speech habits leaves only positive creative speech that helps others and yourself.

ii. ***Right action***: Performing only actions that do not harm self or others. Right action means to abstain from killing or harming other beings, from taking what has not been given and abstaining from sexual misconduct.

iii. ***Right livelihood***: This means that one earns a living by means that involve right thought, speech and action. In other words your livelihood should not harm self or others.

The second division of the Dhamma is Samadhi. Another three parts of the path are included here.

iv. ***Right effort***: In order to prevent unwholesome mental states from arising and to eradicate the unwholesome states that have arisen, also to develop wholesome mental states and maintain those wholesome states and to bring them to full maturity, you generate will, make strong efforts, stir up your energy, apply your mind to it and strive. You must strive to keep your mind in a wholesome place and use your power of focus to bring the wholesome state to full maturity, lasting peace, calm and real happiness.

v. ***Right awareness:*** The awareness of the reality here and now in the present moment. You have begun to become aware of the reality of the moment your breath comes in or goes out! Later you will learn to be aware of the entire reality from the gross to the subtle levels.

vi. ***Right concentration:*** You practice Anapana meditation or breath meditation to sharpen your power of focus and ability to stay focused. It is practice in taming the monkey mind and thereby exerting control over the thoughts that you think. This concentration must have a base of purity, not of craving or aversion. So the breath is used because it is pure; it is just there. There is no need to crave for more breath as the body will automatically breathe, no need to develop aversion, as you need the breath to live.

In the division of Panna are the last two parts of the Noble Eightfold Path.

vii. ***Right thought:*** Your pattern of thinking will gradually change from thoughts of violence, jealousy or negativity to thoughts of wholesomeness, health, positive change and wellbeing.

viii. ***Right understanding:*** Understanding reality As It Is, not as it appears to be or how you would like it to be. You can get an acquired understanding of reality by reading books or listening to others. You can gain an intellectual understanding by examining these words to see if they are rational or make sense to you. But real understanding only comes with experiential knowledge of the subject of reality. Actually experiencing the nature of this mind/body phenomenon within this mind/body phenomenon gives real wisdom. That is right understanding.

The Buddha And Vipassasana Meditation

The Buddha, Sidhartha Gotama, became enlightened when he was 35years old and spent his entire life serving others in the teaching of The Path Of Dhamma until he died at the age of 80. Gotama had tried many, many techniques which were supposed to lead to enlightenment in his day, including self-deprivation to the point of near starvation, but to no avail. He decided to work out his own liberation.

Gotama sat under a tree to meditate with the intention that he would not change his posture or get up for any reason until he reached the stage of full enlightenment. He had already reached very deep levels of concentration and understanding in his previous meditation practice, but he knew he was not yet enlightened and was determined to find the way.

When he emerged from under the tree, he was enlightened, and those who surrounded him testified to this. He had not a trace of anger or negativity left in his being and what he taught his followers was invaluable.

What The Buddha discovered was the role of the bodily sensations in keeping us in a state of reaction to our surroundings and in keeping us rolling in a constant state of craving and aversion toward sensations. Most of our actions are really our re-actions to sensations on the body, pleasant or unpleasant, resulting in a constant state of craving or aversion to our experiences. He also discovered the way to purify the mind. Vipassana Meditation is a process of detangling the mental patterns that create the cycle of attachment and clinging to mind and matter and therefore the cycle of rebirth.

'Vipassana' means 'To observe self, as it is.' Vipassana is a technique that allows all of the past mental conditioning to arise and pass away through the *equanimous* observation of sensations within the body.

We observe uncomfortable sensations arising on the body during meditation and do not react, thus releasing the pattern of the mind to react with aversion. The knowledge of *anicca* or the constant changing of all things, especially as it pertains to the body sensations is also paramount to the effectiveness of the technique. It is easier to let go of any aversion, or resistance when you know that your experience is changing every moment.

The vibrations of all things are constantly changing as well. It is a mistake to get attached to anything of a physical nature, including feelings, because of this constant change we experience every moment. Energy is constantly in motion. Nothing is static. Nothing is innately good or bad. There's just stuff, physical and nonphysical, and our judgment of the stuff. Take out our judgment and we have clear vision. Observe yourself.

Hopefully I have given you enough of a taste of what Vipassana is, for those of you who are seeking this type of experience to be saying YES, that's for me. Vipassana is taught all over the world at 10-day silent retreats. It is a technique to purify the mind and is to this day the most powerful experience of my life and one that has helped me untie many knots in my thought patterns and beliefs; something that I had not been able to achieve despite much effort and determination.

At the 10-day retreat you begin by learning Anapana meditation and after three days you are introduced to Vipassana which is a technique of observation of the bodily sensations. While you are observing your sensations you become aware of Anicca or the constant arising and passing away of sensations which leads to deeper and deeper levels of understanding this mind/body phenomenon.

Some people think that it would be too hard not to talk for ten days. But really, every person I have asked about this at the end of a course says that this quiet is very comforting and not difficult at all to achieve. So don't let that put you off!

This form of meditation may call to you and for those of you who feel drawn to know more about Vipassana Meditation, please visit www.dhamma.org to find a centre near you.

Who Am I to Judge?

Staying out of judgment of yourself and others is so important to experiencing real calm in your life, morning, noon or night.

An untroubled mind,
No longer seeking to consider
What is right and what is wrong,
A mind beyond judgments,
Watches and understands.
The Buddha

As soon as you make a judgment that something is wrong, you create tension within you and you begin to search for ways you can get others to change so that IT is right again, or so that you can feel better again. This is a futile cycle, chasing your tail. You cannot change others to suit you, or your government or the 'system' and even if you succeed for a little while, someone else is working just as hard to change it back and sooner or later they will.

Is this the kind of happiness or calm you seek? A happiness that depends on what others do? Or have you lived enough life to know for yourself that there is an alternative? You can cultivate your own calm from within, shine it out into the world and show others how they too can be happy and fulfilled despite what others in the world are choosing for themselves.

If others are choosing things you do not like, let that be *their* experience. Be light about it and know that your life is about far more important and purposeful issues for you. Let others choose their own reality because ultimately it will serve them by bringing them to a place where they can no longer avoid their own growth. They will have to face their 'stuff' sooner or later. Sooner is always better because you can achieve wonderful peace and lasting health by looking at the things that you feel bad about in your life and making peace with them or making the changes you know you need to make for your own wellness.

Seek To Change From The Inside Out

People often do not intentionally seek to change physically or mentally until they are in pain. When you are in enough physical or mental pain, you finally decide to quit smoking or eat more healthy food or exercise or deal with the mountain of resentment you have been dragging around with you your whole life! That resentment is stored in your physical body and will be reflected in your state of physical health. This is well documented. (((For a great read see *Women's Bodies Women's Wisdom* by Christianne Northrup.)

Or the well known and respected *You Can Heal Your Life* by Louise Hay.

The health of your physical body is intimately connected to your mental and spiritual health. This body is a representation of your spiritual self. It is a symbol of how you are feeling on the inside. Do you feel powerful? Your body shows it. Do you feel angry? Your body represents this somehow with physical signs. Do you feel powerless? Your body shows you by being in a state of ill health that you seemingly cannot control. Do you feel purposeful and joyful? How's your body doing?? I bet I know.

When you are living in the powerful state of knowing that you are creating your experiences and you can now choose your own outlook and responses to life, your body cannot help but be radiantly healthy. If you look at your current state of ill health and kick yourself for not creating a better one, you have not understood properly. Be gentle with yourself.

The present moment only seems to be the real 'reality.' In actuality, this moment has come about as a result of your previous habit patterns. Whatever your life looks like right now is actually the past! All of this is changing now because you are doing very powerful work for the positive. You have been working with these processes for cultivating your morning calm and you have been creating a more calm and joyful future for yourself. Soon you will find yourself stepping into those moments you have created that we call the present!

What you see around you is the effect of what has been thought upon previously. What is yet to

> *come will be the effect of present thought. How important is it then, to rest the mind upon the world you desire, the world that is molding itself even now in response to your brilliant mind's focus?* *Mary Mac*

What Else Do You Want??

The fun thing about this metaphor of the garden we have been creating is that the garden of calm can really be the garden of anything your heart desires! Let's say you want something unusual like to be radiantly beautiful...... Put that into your formula for growing a garden.

Let's look at the causes of 'beauty.' **Awareness of the moment** will allow you to experience absolute truth, the truth that who and what you are IS beauty personified! **Knowing Who You Really Are:** Aka HUMAN GENIUS CREATOR is a definite cause for knowing your beauty! And being in a state of **Non-judgment** is a very important factor for cultivating your knowledge of your own beauty. This is because you need to come at the topic of 'beauty' from a new perspective. Not one that judges beauty by the size of your waist or your proximity to resembling a supermodel. Begin to be open to the different ways that people are beautiful.

Your garden bed should be well prepared already from working with 'the calm,' so you have a good start. Go back and do your **self-talk exercise** to get an idea what your habitual thoughts are about your own beauty. See what you are feeding yourself. **Ask your Inner Being** what you need to know or to do in order to realize your own beauty. Listen with your whole being for the answers. Feel for them.

Do your **self-appreciation exercise** and write down everything you appreciate about yourself and every single way you are beautiful already. These are your seeds of appreciation. Do the **intention exercise** and work out your intentions for yourself and how you feel about you. Change the negative messages into seeds that come from your self-appreciation and will grow the kinds of fruits you desire. Make a list of them so you can remind yourself every day what you intend to create for yourself and what you appreciate about your life. Plant your seeds in your conscious and subconscious throughout your day whenever you remember.

Cultivate the knowledge of your beauty with your **twice daily feedings**. Feed your garden of beauty morning and night with **Meditation, Appreciation** of the day and **Intention** for your restful sleep or your new life experience.

Remember the **Three R's.** When you are in the middle of a negative reaction regarding self-image or beauty first **Relax**. Just accept that you just had a 'moment.' You will automatically let go of some of the negativity just by doing that. Then **Remind** yourself what you want. Have one of your faithful thought-seeds ready for planting, one you know brings you relief. Instead of saying, "I want to be beautiful," which draws your attention to the ways you feel you are not, say something like, "I want to know my own beauty!" Smile to yourself. **Refocus** on your moment, whatever it was you were doing when the negativity arose. Bring beauty into the moment with you. Well done.

Harvest time can hold lots of **self knowledge** for you. You will see how your choice of focus decides what you experience..... Some seeds take longer to sprout and finally fruit than others. The topic of beauty was a big one for me because I had told myself from a very early age that I was fat and ugly. Every time I looked in a mirror, I told myself that. Even at a point in my life that I was actually underweight, I still had times I'd feel fat, so deep was my judgment of myself.

It may take more than one or two affirmations for you to believe in the beauty that stares back at you in the mirror. I have spent many years reprogramming myself and the habit pattern of my mind. But I can now look in a mirror and say, "What a gorgeous creature you are!" Go to the mirror and say that to yourself right now! I dare you. Can you do it? Isn't it interesting to watch yourself?

When you are absolutely sure about your own internal beauty, and I don't mean your blood and bones, I mean your beauty as a powerful, creative being here on planet Earth and elsewhere……. When you are sure of your beauty, you **feel** your beauty, you look in the mirror and have no problem saying to yourself, "What a beautiful creature I am," you become beautiful to everyone else. Your body will come into alignment with your knowledge of your true beauty. It has to! It has no choice because your body is simply a representation of your thoughts, your knowings. You will look radiant and beautiful to others because everyone else in this interesting world of illusion is simply a reflection of YOU. They just reflect back at you how you are feeling about you.

Think about it. Take your journal out and write a name at the top of someone who is in your life, someone meaningful like a family member or close friend. Think about that person and write down their characteristics. Now think about you in relation to those characteristics. The ones you judge as bad are usually either the mirror of what you ARE, meaning you also display this characteristic in some way, or the mirror of what you JUDGE, meaning the characteristic you judge negatively and think people should not be that way.

This judgment, of course, hinders your happiness because every time you come across a person with that characteristic, you feel irritated or angry or self-righteous. Next time someone presents you with a bad vibe, stop and think for a second. How is that reflecting how you were just feeling or what you were just thinking? Say thanks for the reminder!!

Then there is that other unusual desire. Money. Remember to ask yourself what money represents to you. Depending on what your answer is, plug that into your formula for creating a garden of that quality. Money is just the representation of what you really want. So plugging in 'money' will only create resistance for you and in most cases remind you of what you do not have. Plug in 'security' or 'self worth' or 'respect' or 'abundance' and cultivate that.

When you have created that quality within yourself, your life cannot help but present you with the representation of that quality for you, namely, dollars. However, be careful not to TRY to feel abundant so that the dollars will come! Cultivate feelings of abundance until the dollars become irrelevant to you! Am I making sense? I do to me, but since you cannot answer, I wont know until I see if these little books start selling themselves and circulating around the physical plane. That's what I see happening.

When you are absolutely 100% sure about your own value to this world you cannot help but be rich in every way.

Here in the physical, money is simply a symbol representing worth. Your worth. However, that is not to say that every rich person knows his real worth to the world. There are many ways you can be poor and still have lots of money. You can have poor health, poor relationships, feel empty, purposeless. That's not real abundance no matter how many dollars you have.

Always know that it is the inner abundance which we seek as humans. It is the knowledge of our own innate abundance we long to remember. We keep seeking the representational form of this abundance throughout our lives here in this Matrix of reality.

We may think we want calm all around us in the morning, calm children, calm happenings, but we really seek the internal experience of calm and when we have that, the outer experience looks more and more like that. The actual events may even be the same, a bit of this and a bit of that, but your outlook on them will be such that they seem harmonious. You will not need your physical reality to look a certain way in order for you to be whatever you choose to be. This is true power. And you are that.

You don't want to cultivate the morning calm with the intention of others acting differently in the morning! This is an easy mistake to make and a subtle understanding isn't it? You must cultivate the morning calm for only one reason; so that you *feel better*; so that what you radiate out to the rest of the world is a vibration of calm, of love. Be the calm, so that what is happening around you is of no consequence to your state of being. Remember who you are. Remember your power. Temet Nosce. Know thyself. Remember the Law of

Nature. As you sow so shall you reap. Plant your seeds of life with wisdom. Be happy.

I have heard that those who celebrate life
walk safely among the wild animals.
When they go into battle, they remain unharmed.
The animals find no place to attack them
and the weapons are unable to harm them.
Why? Because they can find no place for death in them.
Tao Te Ching (50)

Celebrate Your Life **Geoffrey Brady**

No money in my pockets and my jeans are torn
My hands are cold but my heart is warm
I got somethin money can't buy
Something inside me is comin alive
I got, CELEBRATION, OH OH OH
CELEBRATION OH OH OH

Celebrate YourLife (Celebrate your life)
Celebrate Your Life (Celebrate your life)

Old Man Trouble won't get me down
Nothin you do's gonna turn me around!
The path is narrow but the way is clear
In the distance a sound I hear of

CELEBRATION OH OH OH, CELEBRATION OH OH OH

Celebrate Your Life! (Celebrate your life)
Celebrate Your Life! (Celebrate your life)

You and me, can't you see? We're one big family.
Open your eyes and you'll see, now is the time..... For a

CELEBRATION OH OH OH, CELEBRATION OH OH OH

Celebrate Your Life (Celebrate your life)

LIFE LIFE, Celebrate your LIFE LIFE Celebrate your LIFE
LIFE Celebrate your LIFE LIFE Celebrate your life!

I Choose Love **Mary Mac**

I've known you forever
And we've always been together
I've never met you yet I know you well
Deja vue is my guiding angel.

I am you in this life
And we'll all know truth in this life
The cycles of life spin us around and around again
The choice is yours each and every moment
Round and around and around and around again.

Every moment holds perfection
Between you and your reflection
Evolution requires love
You know how to rise above!

I choose love in this life
You can too in this life
The cycles of life spin us around and around again
The choice is yours each and every moment
Round and around and around and around again.

Every moment holds perfection
Between you and your reflection
Evolution requires love
You know how to rise above!

I choose love in this life!

Affirming Statements

Regarding The Morning Calm

I am the creator of my life!
I can be anything I choose to be.
I choose to be calm and joyful in my daily life.
No one else has to change for me to be happy!
I don't even have to change for me to be happy. I love and accept myself as I am!
But I want to change..... And I know I can change.
I feel the power of my life now.
I am always in the right place at the right time.
Time stands still in my car! (No joke this works for me!)
This situation/feeling won't last forever.
My life unfolds with perfect precision, everything in the right place at the right time.
The river of life is taking me where I want to go.
I just need to "Let go of the oars!" (An Abrahamism)
This will also change. Anicca.
My emotions are a blessing. Thank you.
I am organzsed and on time when I choose to be!

When Feeling Negativity (Resistance) While Focused On Another

People are all different; it makes life interesting.
All perspectives are valuable.
Maybe she is just having a bad day.
I don't know what might have happened to this person.
We are all in the same boat.
S/he is a part of my stream.
We are all one in this web of life.
What is s/he showing me about myself?
S/he wants to be happy too.

Resistance-Releasers Around Relationships

My most important relationship is with myself.
He is on his way to me. She is on her way to me.
Love is a matter of choice and focus.
I choose to love!
My life unfolds with perfect precision.
The Universe is concocting the perfect 'mix' for me.
When I am really ready, I will see her/him.
My partner is a reflectiion of myself. What do I see in him/her?
What do I love about you?
What do I love about me?

Some Thoughts To Release Resistance Around Death And Fear

Death is an illusion.

Death is a natural transition.

Death is a part of life! How could it be bad?

I am only afraid because I do not see clearly.

I choose to see clearly now.

There is only love.

There is only Nature taking its course.

The Universe always looks after me if I let it!

I am safe.

I Choose Life!

New Thoughts To Nourish My Body

My body is incredible just how it is. It's a magnificent machine!

This is my present body! It is always changing.

This body is a perfect reflection of who I am today and that's pretty special!

In many ways I am already extremely happy in this body.

This amazing body is such a privilege to be in here on earth.

This body is very powerful.

My body is the reason I can experience such a joyful life.

My body is the vessel through which Life Force flows.

The happier I get, the more my body comes into alignment with who I really am.

This body is a magnificent self-healing organism!
I am so lucky to be here.
My body knows what it is doing.
This is the perfect body for me today.
This body is the representation of my energetic self!
Now I know what to do with my energy, my body will have to transform too!

Regarding Your Children

I am always doing better than I think.
I am doing just fine.
My children are powerful beings and I am proud of their strength.
It won't always be like this!
My kids are beautiful, creative and powerful beings.
My kids have their own purpose.
My kids have their own guidance.
I am doing the best that I know how at this moment and
My best keeps getting better and better!

I AM HUMAN GENIUS CREATOR- The most empowering statement ever.

References

Hicks, Esther and Jerry, 2004, ***Ask and It Is Given; Learning to Manifest Your Desires,*** Hay House Australia Pty. Ltd., Sydney, NSW.

Contact Abraham-Hicks: P.O. Box 690070 San Antonio, TX 78269 Phone: (830) 755-2299.

Hicks, Esther and Jerry, 2004, ***The Law of Attraction: The Basics of the Teachings of Abraham,*** *2006,* Hay House Australia Pty. Ltd., Sydney, NSW.

Vipassana Research Institute, 1996, ***Mahasatipatthana Sutta; The Great Discourse on the Establishing of Awareness,*** Seattle, WA, USA.

That which offers no resistance,
overcomes the hardest of substances.
That which offers no resistance
can enter where there is no space.
Tao Te Ching (43)

ABOUT THE AUTHOR

Mary Mac is a Life Coach and Workshop Facilitator in Adelaide, South Australia. She specializes in Personal Development, *Health and Wellness* and Life Transitions Coaching with her main area of inspiration being those beings who are on the brink of personal transformation and understanding who they really are and what they came here for. Recently Mary has been developing a program she calls *The Mothershift* for pregnant women and new mums to help them develop the mental strength and clarity they need for the epic journey ahead!

Mary is also an inspiring musician whose original music and lyrics tell the stories of her own personal transformation from who she really wasn't to who she really is. She aims to inspire others through this 'Magic We Call Life' to their own intimate connection with All That Is and the key to creating a life of OUTRAGEOUS JOY! To contact Mary and find out about future workshops, books, CDs or Life Coaching please use the following information.

P.O. Box 2021

Magill North, SA 5068

Australia

0429 013 359

www.marymccloud.com.au

Mary Mac

Cultivate The Morning Calm

www.ingramcontent.com/pod-product-compliance
Ingram Content Group UK Ltd.
Pitfield, Milton Keynes, MK11 3LW, UK
UKHW020220250726
13967UKWH00001B/113

9 781300 141631